PLAYS BY AUGUST STRINDBERG • STRINDBERG, AUGUST

Publisher's Note

Purchase of this book entitles you to a free trial membership in the publisher's book club at www.rarebooksclub.com. (Time limited offer.) Simply enter the barcode number from the back cover onto the membership form on our home page. The book club entitles you to select from millions of books at no additional charge. You can also download a digital copy of this and related books to read on the go. Simply enter the title or subject onto the search form to find them.

Note: This is an historic book. Pages numbers, where present in the text, refer to the first edition of the book. The table of contents or index may also refer to them.

If you have any questions, could you please be so kind as to consult our Frequently Asked Questions page at www.rarebooksclub.com/faqs.cfm? You are also welcome to contact us there.

Publisher: General Books LLC™, Memphis, TN, USA, 2012. ISBN: 9781153737210.

Credits: Distributed Proofreaders.

❧ ❧ ❧ ❧ ❧ ❧ ❧ ❧

PLAYS BY

AUGUST STRINDBERG

CREDITORS PARIAH

TRANSLATED FROM THE SWEDISH, WITH INTRODUCTIONS BY EDWIN BJORKMAN

CREDITORS

INTRODUCTION

This is one of the three plays which Strindberg placed at the head of his dramatic production during the middle ultra-naturalistic period, the other two being "The Father" and "Miss Julia." It is, in many ways, one of the strongest he ever produced. Its rarely excelled unity of construction, its tremendous dramatic tension, and its wonderful psychological analysis combine to make it a masterpiece.

In Swedish its name is "Fordringsagare." This indefinite form may be either singular or plural, but it is rarely used except as a plural. And the play itself makes it perfectly clear that the proper translation of its title is "Creditors," for under this aspect appear both the former and the present husband of Tekla. One of the main objects of the play is to reveal her indebtedness first to one and then to the other of these men, while all the time she is posing as a person of original gifts.

I have little doubt that Strindberg, at the time he wrote this play—and bear in mind that this happened only a year before he finally decided to free himself from an impossible marriage by an appeal to the law—believed Tekla to be fairly representative of womanhood in general. The utter unreasonableness of such a view need hardly be pointed out, and I shall waste no time on it. A question more worthy of discussion is whether the figure of Tekla be true to life merely as the picture of a personality—as one out of numerous imaginable variations on a type decided not by sex but by faculties and qualities. And the same question may well be raised in regard to the two men, both of whom are evidently intended to win our sympathy: one as the victim of a fate stronger than himself, and the other as the conqueror of adverse and humiliating circumstances.

Personally, I am inclined to doubt whether a Tekla can be found in the flesh—and even if found, she might seem too exceptional to gain acceptance as a real individuality. It must be remembered, however, that, in spite of his avowed realism, Strindberg did not draw his men and women in the spirit generally designated as impressionistic; that is, with the idea that they might step straight from his pages into life and there win recognition as human beings of familiar aspect. His realism is always mixed with idealism; his figures are always "doctored," so to speak. And they have been thus treated in order to enable their creator to drive home the particular truth he is just then concerned with.

Consciously or unconsciously he sought to produce what may be designated as "pure cultures" of certain human qualities. But these he took great pains to arrange in their proper psychological settings, for mental and moral qualities, like everything else, run in groups that are more or less harmonious, if not exactly homogeneous. The man with a single quality, like Moliere's Harpagon, was much too primitive and crude for Strindberg's art, as he himself rightly asserted in his preface to "Miss Julia." When he wanted to draw the genius of greed, so to speak, he did it by setting it in the midst of related qualities of a kind most likely to be attracted by it.

Tekla is such a "pure culture" of a group of naturally correlated mental and moral qualities and functions and tendencies—of a personality built up logically around a dominant central note. There are within all of us many personalities, some of which remain for ever potentialities. But it is conceivable that any one of them, under circumstances different from those in which we have been living, might have developed into its severely logical consequence—or, if you please, into a human being that would be held abnormal if actually encountered.

This is exactly what Strindberg seems to have done time and again, both in his middle and final periods, in his novels as well as in his plays. In all of us a Tekla, an Adolph, a Gustav—or a Jean and a Miss Julia—be more or less dormant. And if we search our souls unsparingly, I fear the result can only be an admission that—had the needed set of circumstances been provided—we might have come unpleasantly close to one of those Strindbergian creatures which we are now inclined to reject as unhuman.

Here we have the secret of what I believe to be the great Swedish dramatist's strongest hold on our interest. How could it otherwise happen that so many critics, of such widely differing temperaments, have recorded identical feelings as springing from a study of his work: on one side an active resentment, a keen unwillingness to be interested; on the other, an attraction that would not be denied in spite of resolute resistance to it! For Strindberg DOES hold us, even when we regret his power of doing so. And no one familiar with the conclusions of modern psychology could imagine such a paradox possible did not the object of our sorely divided feelings provide us with something that our minds instinctively recognise as true to life in some way, and for that reason valuable to the art of living.

There are so many ways of presenting truth. Strindberg's is only one of them—and not the one commonly employed nowadays. Its main fault lies perhaps in being too intellectual, too abstract. For while Strindberg was intensely emotional, and while this fact colours all his writings, he could only express himself through his reason. An emotion that would move another man to murder would precipitate Strindberg into merciless analysis of his own or somebody else's mental and moral make-up. At any rate, I do not proclaim his way of presenting truth as the best one of all available. But I suspect that this decidedly strange way of Strindberg's—resulting in such repulsively superior beings as Gustav, or in such grievously inferior ones as Adolph—may come nearer the temper and needs of the future than do the ways of much more plausible writers. This does not need to imply that the future will imitate Strindberg. But it may ascertain what he aimed at doing, and then do it with a degree of perfection which he, the pioneer, could never hope to attain.

CREDITORS

A TRAGICOMEDY
1889

PERSONS

TEKLA
ADOLPH, her husband, a painter
GUSTAV, her divorced husband, a high-school teacher (who is travelling under an assumed name)

SCENE

(A parlor in a summer hotel on the seashore. The rear wall has a door opening on a veranda, beyond which is seen a landscape. To the right of the door stands a table with newspapers on it. There is a chair on the left side of the stage. To the right of the table stands a sofa. A door on the right leads to an adjoining room.)

(ADOLPH and GUSTAV, the latter seated on the sofa by the table to the right.)

ADOLPH. [At work on a wax figure on a miniature modelling stand; his crutches are placed beside him]—and for all this I have to thank you!

GUSTAV. [Smoking a cigar] Oh, nonsense!

ADOLPH. Why, certainly! During the first days after my wife had gone, I lay helpless on a sofa and did nothing but long for her. It was as if she had taken away my crutches with her, so that I couldn't move from the spot. When I had slept a couple of days, I seemed to come to, and began to pull myself together. My head calmed down after having been working feverishly. Old thoughts from days gone by bobbed up again. The desire to work and the instinct for creation came back. My eyes recovered their faculty of quick and straight vision—and then you showed up.

GUSTAV. I admit you were in a miserable condition when I first met you, and you had to use your crutches when you walked, but this is not to say that my presence has been the cause of your recovery. You needed a rest, and you had a craving for masculine company.

ADOLPH. Oh, that's true enough, like everything you say. Once I used to have men for friends, but I thought them superfluous after I married, and I felt quite satisfied with the one I had chosen. Later I was drawn into new circles and made a lot of acquaintances, but my wife was jealous of them—she wanted to keep me to herself: worse still—she wanted also to keep my friends to herself. And so I was left alone with my own jealousy.

GUSTAV. Yes, you have a strong tendency toward that kind of disease.

ADOLPH. I was afraid of losing her—and I tried to prevent it. There is nothing strange in that. But I was never afraid that she might be deceiving me—

GUSTAV. No, that's what married men are never afraid of.

ADOLPH. Yes, isn't it queer? What I really feared was that her friends would get such an influence over her that they would begin to exercise some kind of indirect power over me—and THAT is something I couldn't bear.

GUSTAV. So your ideas don't agree—yours and your wife's?

ADOLPH. Seeing that you have heard so much already, I may as well tell you everything. My wife has an independent nature—what are you smiling at?

GUSTAV. Go on! She has an independent nature—

ADOLPH. Which cannot accept anything from me—

GUSTAV. But from everybody else.

ADOLPH. [After a pause] Yes.—And it looked as if she especially hated my ideas because they were mine, and not because there was anything wrong about them. For it used to happen quite often that she advanced ideas that had once been mine, and that she stood up for them as her own. Yes, it even happened that friends of mine gave her ideas which they had taken directly from me, and then they seemed all right. Everything was all right except what came from me.

GUSTAV. Which means that you are not entirely happy?

ADOLPH. Oh yes, I am happy. I have the one I wanted, and I have never wanted anybody else.

GUSTAV. And you have never wanted to be free?

ADOLPH. No, I can't say that I have. Oh, well, sometimes I have imagined that it might seem like a rest to be free. But the moment she leaves me, I begin to long for her—long for her as for my own arms and legs. It is queer that sometimes I have a feeling that she is nothing in herself, but only a part of myself—an organ that can take away with it my will, my very desire to live. It seems almost as if I had deposited with her that centre of vitality of which the anatomical books tell us.

GUSTAV. Perhaps, when we get to the bottom of it, that is just what has happened.

ADOLPH. How could it be so? Is she not an independent being, with thoughts of her own? And when I met her I was nothing—a child of an artist whom she undertook to educate.

GUSTAV. But later you developed her thoughts and educated her, didn't you?

ADOLPH. No, she stopped growing and I pushed on.

GUSTAV. Yes, isn't it strange that her "authoring" seemed to fall off after her first book—or that it failed to improve, at least? But that first time she had a subject which wrote itself—for I understand she used her former husband for a model. You never knew him, did you? They say he was an idiot.

ADOLPH. I never knew him, as he was away for six months at a time. But he must have been an arch-idiot, judging by her picture of him. [Pause] And you may feel sure that the picture was correct.

GUSTAV. I do!—But why did she ever take him?

ADOLPH. Because she didn't know him well enough. Of course, you never DO get acquainted until afterward!

GUSTAV. And for that reason one ought not to marry until—afterward.—And he was a tyrant, of course?

ADOLPH. Of course?

GUSTAV. Why, so are all married men. [Feeling his way] And you not the least.

ADOLPH. I? Who let my wife come and go as she pleases—

GUSTAV. Well, that's nothing. You couldn't lock her up, could you? But do you like her to stay away whole nights?

ADOLPH. No, really, I don't.

GUSTAV. There, you see! [With a change of tactics] And to tell the truth, it would only make you ridiculous to like it.

ADOLPH. Ridiculous? Can a man be ridiculous because he trusts his wife?

GUSTAV. Of course he can. And it's just what you are already—and thoroughly at that!

ADOLPH. [Convulsively] I! It's what I dread most of all—and there's going to be a change.

GUSTAV. Don't get excited now—or you'll have another attack.

ADOLPH. But why isn't she ridiculous when I stay out all night?

GUSTAV. Yes, why? Well, it's nothing that concerns you, but that's the way it is. And while you are trying to figure out why, the mishap has already occurred.

ADOLPH. What mishap?

GUSTAV. However, the first husband was a tyrant, and she took him only to get her freedom. You see, a girl cannot have freedom except by providing herself with a chaperon—or what we call a husband.

ADOLPH. Of course not.

GUSTAV. And now you are the chaperon.

ADOLPH. I?

GUSTAV. Since you are her husband.

(ADOLPH keeps a preoccupied silence.)

GUSTAV. Am I not right?

ADOLPH. [Uneasily] I don't know. You live with a woman for years, and you never stop to analyse her, or your relationship with her, and then—then you begin to think—and there you are!—Gustav, you are my friend. The only male friend I have. During this last week you have given me courage to live again. It is as if your own magnetism had been poured into me. Like a watchmaker, you have fixed the works in my head and wound up the spring again. Can't you hear, yourself, how I think more clearly and speak more to the point? And to myself at least it seems as if my voice had recovered its ring.

GUSTAV. So it seems to me also. And why is that?

ADOLPH. I shouldn't wonder if you grew accustomed to lower your voice in talking to women. I know at least that Tekla always used to accuse me of shouting.

GUSTAV. And so you toned down your voice and accepted the rule of the slipper?

ADOLPH. That isn't quite the way to put it. [After some reflection] I think it is even worse than that. But let us talk of something else!—What was I saying?—Yes, you came here, and you enabled me to see my art in its true light. Of course, for some time I had noticed my growing lack of interest in painting, as it didn't seem to offer me the proper medium for the expression of what I wanted to bring out. But when you explained all this to me, and made it clear why painting must fail as a timely outlet for the creative instinct, then I saw the light at last—and I realised that hereafter it would not be possible for me to express myself by means of colour only.

GUSTAV. Are you quite sure now that you cannot go on painting— that you may not have a relapse?

ADOLPH. Perfectly sure! For I have tested myself. When I went to bed that night after our talk, I rehearsed your argument point by point, and I knew you had it right. But when I woke up from a good night's sleep and my head was clear again, then it came over me in a flash that you might be mistaken after all. And I jumped out of bed and got hold of my brushes and paints—but it was no use! Every trace of illusion was gone—it was nothing but smears of paint, and I quaked at the thought of having believed, and having made others believe, that a painted canvas could be anything but a painted canvas. The veil had fallen from my eyes, and it was just as impossible for me to paint any more as it was to become a child again.

GUSTAV. And then you saw that the realistic tendency of our day, its craving for actuality and tangibility, could only find its proper form in sculpture, which gives you body, extension in all three dimensions—

ADOLPH. [Vaguely] The three dimensions—oh yes, body, in a word!

GUSTAV. And then you became a sculptor yourself. Or rather, you have been one all your life, but you had gone astray, and nothing was needed but a guide to put you on the right road—Tell me, do you experience supreme joy now when you are at work?

ADOLPH. Now I am living!

GUSTAV. May I see what you are doing?

ADOLPH. A female figure.

GUSTAV. Without a model? And so lifelike at that!

ADOLPH. [Apathetically] Yes, but it resembles somebody. It is remarkable that this woman seems to have become a part of my body as I of hers.

GUSTAV. Well, that's not so very remarkable. Do you know what transfusion is?

ADOLPH. Of blood? Yes.

GUSTAV. And you seem to have bled yourself a little too much. When I look at the figure here I comprehend several things which I merely guessed before. You have loved her tremendously!

ADOLPH. Yes, to such an extent that I couldn't tell whether she was I or I she. When she is smiling, I smile also. When she is weeping, I weep. And when she—can you imagine anything like it?— when she was giving life to our child—I felt the birth pangs within myself.

GUSTAV. Do you know, my dear friend—I hate to speak of it, but you are already showing the first symptoms of epilepsy.

ADOLPH. [Agitated] I! How can you tell?

GUSTAV. Because I have watched the symptoms in a younger brother of mine who had been worshipping Venus a little too excessively.

ADOLPH. How—how did it show itself—that thing you spoke of?

[During the following passage GUSTAV speaks with great animation, and ADOLPH listens so intently that, unconsciously, he imitates many of GUSTAV'S gestures.]

GUSTAV. It was dreadful to witness, and if you don't feel strong enough I won't inflict a description of it on you.

ADOLPH. [Nervously] Yes, go right on—just go on!

GUSTAV. Well, the boy happened to marry an innocent little creature with curls, and eyes like a turtle-dove; with the face of a child and the pure soul of an angel. But nevertheless she managed to usurp the male prerogative—

ADOLPH. What is that?

GUSTAV. Initiative, of course. And with the result that the angel nearly carried him off to heaven. But first he had to be put on the cross and made to feel the nails in his flesh. It was horrible!

ADOLPH. [Breathlessly] Well, what happened?

GUSTAV. [Lingering on each word] We might be sitting together talking, he and I—and when I had been speaking for a while his face would turn white as chalk, his arms and legs would grow stiff, and his thumbs became twisted against the palms of his hands—like this. [He illustrates the movement and it is imitated by ADOLPH] Then his eyes became bloodshot, and he began to chew— like this. [He chews, and again ADOLPH imitates him] The saliva was rattling in his throat. His chest was squeezed together as if it had been closed in a vice. The pupils of his eyes flickered like gas-jets. His tongue beat the saliva into a lather, and he sank— slowly—down—backward—into the chair—as if he were drowning. And then—-

ADOLPH. [In a whisper] Stop now!

GUSTAV. And then—Are you not feeling well?

ADOLPH. No.

GUSTAV. [Gets a glass of water for him] There: drink now. And we'll talk of something else.

ADOLPH. [Feebly] Thank you! Please go on!

GUSTAV. Well—when he came to he couldn't remember anything at all. He had simply lost consciousness. Has that ever happened to you?

ADOLPH. Yes, I have had attacks of vertigo now and then, but my physician says it's only anaemia.

GUSTAV. Well, that's the beginning of it, you know. But, believe me, it will end in epilepsy if you don't take care of yourself.

ADOLPH. What can I do?

GUSTAV. To begin with, you will have to observe complete abstinence.

ADOLPH. For how long?

GUSTAV. For half a year at least.

ADOLPH. I cannot do it. That would upset our married life.

GUSTAV. Good-bye to you then!

ADOLPH. [Covers up the wax figure] I cannot do it!

GUSTAV. Can you not save your own life?—But tell me, as you have already given me so much of your confidence—is there no other canker, no secret wound, that troubles you? For it is very rare to find only one cause of discord, as life is so full of variety and so fruitful in chances for false relationships. Is there not a corpse in your cargo that you are trying to hide from yourself?— For instance, you said a minute ago that you have a child which has been left in other people's care. Why don't you keep it with you?

ADOLPH. My wife doesn't want us to do so.

GUSTAV. And her reason? Speak up now!

ADOLPH. Because, when it was about three years old, it began to look like him, her former husband.

GUSTAV. Well? Have you seen her former husband?

ADOLPH. No, never. I have only had a casual glance at a very poor portrait of him, and then I couldn't detect the slightest resemblance.

GUSTAV. Oh, portraits are never like the original, and, besides, he might have changed considerably since it was made. However, I hope it hasn't aroused any suspicions in you?

ADOLPH. Not at all. The child was born a year after our marriage, and the husband was abroad when I first met Tekla—it happened right here, in this very house even, and that's why we come here every summer.

GUSTAV. No, then there can be no

cause for suspicion. And you wouldn't have had any reason to trouble yourself anyhow, for the children of a widow who marries again often show a likeness to her dead husband. It is annoying, of course, and that's why they used to burn all widows in India, as you know.—But tell me: have you ever felt jealous of him—of his memory? Would it not sicken you to meet him on a walk and hear him, with his eyes on your Tekla, use the word "we" instead of "I"?—We!

ADOLPH. I cannot deny that I have been pursued by that very thought.

GUSTAV. There now!—And you'll never get rid of it. There are discords in this life which can never be reduced to harmony. For this reason you had better put wax in your ears and go to work. If you work, and grow old, and pile masses of new impressions on the hatches, then the corpse will stay quiet in the hold.

ADOLPH. Pardon me for interrupting you, but—it is wonderful how you resemble Tekla now and then while you are talking. You have a way of blinking one eye as if you were taking aim with a gun, and your eyes have the same influence on me as hers have at times.

GUSTAV. No, really?

ADOLPH. And now you said that "no, really" in the same indifferent way that she does. She also has the habit of saying "no, really" quite often.

GUSTAV. Perhaps we are distantly related, seeing that all human beings are said to be of one family. At any rate, it will be interesting to make your wife's acquaintance to see if what you say is true.

ADOLPH. And do you know, she never takes an expression from me. She seems rather to avoid my vocabulary, and I have never caught her using any of my gestures. And yet people as a rule develop what is called "marital resemblance."

GUSTAV. And do you know why this has not happened in your case?—That woman has never loved you.

ADOLPH. What do you mean?

GUSTAV. I hope you will excuse what I am saying—but woman's love consists in taking, in receiving, and one from whom she takes nothing does not have her love. She has never loved you!

ADOLPH. Don't you think her capable of loving more than once?

GUSTAV. No, for we cannot be deceived more than once. Then our eyes are opened once for all. You have never been deceived, and so you had better beware of those that have. They are dangerous, I tell you.

ADOLPH. Your words pierce me like knife thrusts, and I feel as if something were being severed within me, but I cannot help it. And this cutting brings a certain relief, too. For it means the pricking of ulcers that never seemed to ripen.—She has never loved me!—Why, then, did she ever take me?

GUSTAV. Tell me first how she came to take you, and whether it was you who took her or she who took you?

ADOLPH. Heaven only knows if I can tell at all!—How did it happen? Well, it didn't come about in one day.

GUSTAV. Would you like to have me tell you how it did happen?

ADOLPH. That's more than you can do.

GUSTAV. Oh, by using the information about yourself and your wife that you have given me, I think I can reconstruct the whole event. Listen now, and you'll hear. [In a dispassionate tone, almost humorously] The husband had gone abroad to study, and she was alone. At first her freedom seemed rather pleasant. Then came a sense of vacancy, for I presume she was pretty empty when she had lived by herself for a fortnight. Then he appeared, and by and by the vacancy was filled up. By comparison the absent one seemed to fade out, and for the simple reason that he was at a distance—you know the law about the square of the distance? But when they felt their passions stirring, then came fear—of themselves, of their consciences, of him. For protection they played brother and sister. And the more their feelings smacked of the flesh, the more they tried to make their relationship appear spiritual.

ADOLPH. Brother and sister? How could you know that?

GUSTAV. I guessed it. Children are in the habit of playing papa and mamma, but when they grow up they play brother and sister—in order to hide what should be hidden!—And then they took the vow of chastity—and then they played hide-and-seek—until they got in a dark corner where they were sure of not being seen by anybody. [With mock severity] But they felt that there was ONE whose eye reached them in the darkness—and they grew frightened—and their fright raised the spectre of the absent one—his figure began to assume immense proportions—it became metamorphosed: turned into a nightmare that disturbed their amorous slumbers; a creditor who knocked at all doors. Then they saw his black hand between their own as these sneaked toward each other across the table; and they heard his grating voice through that stillness of the night that should have been broken only by the beating of their own pulses. He did not prevent them from possessing each other but he spoiled their happiness. And when they became aware of his invisible interference with their happiness; when they took flight at last—a vain flight from the memories that pursued them, from the liability they had left behind, from the public opinion they could not face—and when they found themselves without the strength needed to carry their own guilt, then they had to send out into the fields for a scapegoat to be sacrificed. They were free-thinkers, but they did not have the courage to step forward and speak openly to him the words: "We love each other!" To sum it up, they were cowards, and so the tyrant had to be slaughtered. Is that right?

ADOLPH. Yes, but you forget that she educated me, that she filled my head with new thoughts—

GUSTAV. I have not forgotten it. But tell me: why could she not educate the other man also—into a free-thinker?

ADOLPH. Oh, he was an idiot!

GUSTAV. Oh, of course—he was an idiot! But that's rather an ambiguous term, and, as pictured in her novel, his idiocy seems mainly to have consisted in failure to understand her. Pardon me a question: but is your wife so very profound after all? I have discovered nothing profound in her writings.

ADOLPH. Neither have I.—But then I have also to confess a certain difficulty in understanding her. It is as if the cogs of our brain wheels didn't fit into each other, and as if something went to pieces in my head when I try to comprehend her.

GUSTAV. Maybe you are an idiot, too?

ADOLPH. I don't THINK so! And it seems to me all the time as if she were in the wrong—Would you care to read this letter, for instance, which I got to-day?

[Takes out a letter from his pocketbook.]

GUSTAV. [Glancing through the letter] Hm! The handwriting seems strangely familiar.

ADOLPH. Rather masculine, don't you think?

GUSTAV. Well, I know at least ONE man who writes that kind of hand—She addresses you as "brother." Are you still playing comedy to each other? And do you never permit yourselves any greater familiarity in speaking to each other?

ADOLPH. No, it seems to me that all mutual respect is lost in that way.

GUSTAV. And is it to make you respect her that she calls herself your sister?

ADOLPH. I want to respect her more than myself. I want her to be the better part of my own self.

GUSTAV. Why don't you be that better part yourself? Would it be less convenient than to permit somebody else to fill the part? Do you want to place yourself beneath your wife?

ADOLPH. Yes, I do. I take a pleasure in never quite reaching up to her. I have taught her to swim, for example, and now I enjoy hearing her boast that she surpasses me both in skill and daring. To begin with, I merely pretended to be awkward and timid in order to raise her courage. And so it ended with my actually being her inferior, more of a coward than she. It almost seemed to me as if she had actually taken my courage away from me.

GUSTAV. Have you taught her anything else?

ADOLPH. Yes—but it must stay between us—I have taught her how to spell, which she didn't know before. But now, listen: when she took charge of our domestic correspondence, I grew out of the habit of writing. And think of it: as the years passed on, lack of practice made me forget a little here and there of my grammar. But do you think she recalls that I was the one who taught her at the start? No—and so I am "the idiot," of course.

GUSTAV. So you are an idiot already?

ADOLPH. Oh, it's just a joke, of course!

GUSTAV. Of course! But this is clear cannibalism, I think. Do you know what's behind that sort of practice? The savages eat their enemies in order to acquire their useful qualities. And this woman has been eating your soul, your courage, your knowledge—-

ADOLPH. And my faith! It was I who urged her to write her first book—-

GUSTAV. [Making a face] Oh-h-h!

ADOLPH. It was I who praised her, even when I found her stuff rather poor. It was I who brought her into literary circles where she could gather honey from our most ornamental literary flowers. It was I who used my personal influence to keep the critics from her throat. It was I who blew her faith in herself into flame; blew on it until I lost my own breath. I gave, gave, gave—until I had nothing left for myself. Do you know—I'll tell you everything now—do you know I really believe—and the human soul is so peculiarly constituted—I believe that when my artistic successes seemed about to put her in the shadow—as well as her reputation—then I tried to put courage into her by belittling myself, and by making my own art seem inferior to hers. I talked so long about the insignificant part played by painting on the whole—talked so long about it, and invented so many reasons to prove what I said, that one fine day I found myself convinced of its futility. So all you had to do was to breathe on a house of cards.

GUSTAV. Pardon me for recalling what you said at the beginning of our talk—that she had never taken anything from you.

ADOLPH. She doesn't nowadays. Because there is nothing more to take.

GUSTAV. The snake being full, it vomits now.

ADOLPH. Perhaps she has been taking a good deal more from me than I have been aware of?

GUSTAV. You can be sure of that. She took when you were not looking, and that is called theft.

ADOLPH. Perhaps she never did educate me?

GUSTAV. But you her? In all likelihood! But it was her trick to make it appear the other way to you. May I ask how she set about educating you?

ADOLPH. Oh, first of all—hm!

GUSTAV. Well?

ADOLPH. Well, I—-

GUSTAV. No, we were speaking of her.

ADOLPH. Really, I cannot tell now.

GUSTAV. Do you see!

ADOLPH. However—she devoured my faith also, and so I sank further and further down, until you came along and gave me a new faith.

GUSTAV. [Smiling] In sculpture?

ADOLPH. [Doubtfully] Yes.

GUSTAV. And have you really faith in it? In this abstract, antiquated art that dates back to the childhood of civilisation? Do you believe that you can obtain your effect by pure form—by the three dimensions—tell me? That you can reach the practical mind of our own day, and convey an illusion to it, without the use of colour—without colour, mind you—do you really believe that?

ADOLPH. [Crushed] No!

GUSTAV. Well, I don't either.

ADOLPH. Why, then, did you say you did?

GUSTAV. Because I pitied you.

ADOLPH. Yes, I am to be pitied! For now I am bankrupt! Finished!—And worst of all: not even she is left to me!

GUSTAV. Well, what could you do with her?

ADOLPH. Oh, she would be to me what God was before I became an atheist: an object that might help me to exercise my sense of veneration.

GUSTAV. Bury your sense of veneration and let something else grow on top of it. A little wholesome scorn, for instance.

ADOLPH. I cannot live without having something to respect—-

GUSTAV. Slave!

ADOLPH.—without a woman to respect and worship!

GUSTAV. Oh, HELL! Then you had better take back your God—if you needs must have something to kow-tow to! You're a fine atheist, with all that superstition about woman still in you! You're a fine free-thinker, who dare not think freely about the dear ladies! Do you know what that incomprehensible, sphinx-like, profound something in your wife really is? It is sheer stupidity!—Look here: she cannot even distinguish between th and t. And that, you know, means there is something wrong with the mechanism. When you look at the case, it looks like a chronometer, but the works inside are those of an ordinary cheap watch.—Nothing but the skirts-that's all! Put trousers on her, give her a pair of moustaches of soot under her nose, then take a good, sober look at her, and listen to her in the same manner: you'll find the instrument has another sound to it. A phonograph, and nothing else—giving you back your own words, or those of other people—and always in diluted form. Have you ever looked at a naked woman- -oh yes, yes, of course! A youth with over-developed breasts; an under-developed man; a child that has shot up to full height and then stopped growing in other respects; one who is chronically anaemic: what can you expect of such a creature?

ADOLPH. Supposing all that to be true—how can it be possible that
I still think her my equal?

GUSTAV. Hallucination—the hypnotising power of skirts! Or—the two of you may actually have become equals. The levelling process has been finished. Her capillarity has brought the water in both tubes to the same height.—Tell me [taking out his watch]: our talk has now lasted six hours, and your wife ought soon to be here. Don't you think we had better stop, so that you can get a rest?

ADOLPH. No, don't leave me! I don't dare to be alone!

GUSTAV. Oh, for a little while only—and then the lady will come.

ADOLPH. Yes, she is coming!—It's all so queer! I long for her, but I am afraid of her. She pets me, she is tender to me, but there is suffocation in her kisses—something that pulls and numbs. And I feel like a circus child that is being pinched by the clown in order that it may look rosy-cheeked when it appears before the public.

GUSTAV. I feel very sorry for you, my friend. Without being a physician, I can tell that you are a dying man. It is enough to look at your latest pictures in order to see that.

ADOLPH. You think so? How can you see it?

GUSTAV. Your colour is watery blue, anaemic, thin, so that the cadaverous yellow of the canvas shines through. And it impresses me as if your own hollow, putty-coloured cheeks were showing beneath—

ADOLPH. Oh, stop, stop!

GUSTAV. Well, this is not only my personal opinion. Have you read today's paper?

ADOLPH. [Shrinking] No!

GUSTAV. It's on the table here.

ADOLPH. [Reaching for the paper without daring to take hold of it]
Do they speak of it there?

GUSTAV. Read it—or do you want me to read it to you?

ADOLPH. No!

GUSTAV. I'll leave you, if you want me to.

ADOLPH. No, no, no!—I don't know—it seems as if I were beginning to hate you, and yet I cannot let you go.—You drag me out of the hole into which I have fallen, but no sooner do you get me on firm ice, than you knock me on the head and shove me into the water again. As long as my secrets were my own, I had still something left within me, but now I am quite empty. There is a canvas by an Italian master, showing a scene of torture—a saint whose intestines are being torn out of him and rolled on the axle of a windlass. The martyr is watching himself grow thinner and thinner, while the roll on the axle grows thicker.—Now it seems to me as if you had swelled out since you began to dig in me; and when you leave, you'll carry away my vitals with you, and leave nothing but an empty shell behind.

GUSTAV. How you do let your fancy run away with you!—And besides, your wife is bringing back your heart.

ADOLPH. No, not since you have burned her to ashes. Everything is in ashes where you have passed along: my art, my love, my hope, my faith!

GUSTAV. All of it was pretty nearly finished before I came along.

ADOLPH. Yes, but it might have been saved. Now it's too late— incendiary!

GUSTAV. We have cleared some ground only. Now we'll sow in the ashes.

ADOLPH. I hate you! I curse you!

GUSTAV. Good symptoms! There is still some strength left in you. And now I'll pull you up on the ice again. Listen now! Do you want to listen to me, and do you want to obey me?

ADOLPH. Do with me what you will—I'll obey you!

GUSTAV. [Rising] Look at me!

ADOLPH. [Looking at GUSTAV] Now you are looking at me again with that other pair of eyes which attracts me.

GUSTAV. And listen to me!

ADOLPH. Yes, but speak of yourself. Don't talk of me any longer I am like an open wound and cannot bear being touched.

GUSTAV. No, there is nothing to say about me. I am a teacher of dead languages, and a widower—that's all! Take my hand.

ADOLPH. What terrible power there must be in you! It feels as if I were touching an electrical generator.

GUSTAV. And bear in mind that I have been as weak as you are now.--Stand up!

ADOLPH. [Rises, but keeps himself from falling only by throwing his arms around the neck of GUSTAV] I am like a boneless baby, and my brain seems to lie bare.

GUSTAV. Take a turn across the floor!

ADOLPH. I cannot!

GUSTAV. Do what I say, or I'll strike you!

ADOLPH. [Straightening himself up] What are you saying?

GUSTAV. I'll strike you, I said.

ADOLPH. [Leaping backward in a rage] You!

GUSTAV. That's it! Now you have got the blood into your head, and your self-assurance is awake. And now I'll give you some electriticy: where is your wife?

ADOLPH. Where is she?

GUSTAV. Yes.

ADOLPH. She is—at—a meeting.

GUSTAV. Sure?

ADOLPH. Absolutely!

GUSTAV. What kind of meeting?

ADOLPH. Oh, something relating to an orphan asylum.

GUSTAV. Did you part as friends?

ADOLPH. [With some hesitation] Not as friends.

GUSTAV. As enemies then!—What did you say that provoked her?

ADOLPH. You are terrible. I am afraid of you. How could you know?

GUSTAV. It's very simple: I possess three known factors, and with their help I figure out the unknown one. What did you say to her?

ADOLPH. I said—two words only, but they were dreadful, and I regret them—regret them very much.

GUSTAV. Don't do it! Tell me now?

ADOLPH. I said: "Old flirt!"

GUSTAV. What more did you say?

ADOLPH. Nothing at all.

GUSTAV. Yes, you did, but you have forgotten it—perhaps because you don't dare remember it. You have put it away in a secret drawer, but you have got to open it now!

ADOLPH. I can't remember!

GUSTAV. But I know. This is what you said: "You ought to be ashamed of flirting when you are too old to have any more lovers!"

ADOLPH. Did I say that? I must have said it!—But how can you know that I did?

GUSTAV. I heard her tell the story on board the boat as I came here.

ADOLPH. To whom?

GUSTAV. To four young men who formed her company. She is already developing a taste for chaste young men, just like—

ADOLPH. But there is nothing wrong in that?

GUSTAV. No more than in playing brother and sister when you are papa and mamma.

ADOLPH. So you have seen her then?

GUSTAV. Yes, I have. But you have never seen her when you didn't— I mean, when you were not present. And there's the reason, you see, why a husband can never really know his wife. Have you a portrait of her?

(Adolph takes a photograph from his pocketbook. There is a look of aroused curiosity on his face.)

GUSTAV. You were not present when this was taken?

ADOLPH. No.

GUSTAV. Look at it. Does it bear much resemblance to the portrait you painted of her? Hardly any! The features are the same, but the expression is quite different. But you don't see this, because your own picture of her creeps in between your eyes and this one. Look at it now as a painter, without giving a thought to the original. What does it represent? Nothing, so far as I can see, but an affected coquette inviting somebody to come and play with her. Do you notice this cynical line around the mouth which you are never allowed to see? Can you see that her eyes are seeking out some man who is not you? Do you observe that her dress is cut low at the neck, that her hair is done up in a different way, that her sleeve has managed to slip back from her arm? Can you see?

ADOLPH. Yes—now I see.

GUSTAV. Look out, my boy!

ADOLPH. For what?

GUSTAV. For her revenge! Bear in mind that when you said she could not attract a man, you struck at what to her is most sacred—the one thing above all others. If you had told her that she wrote nothing but nonsense, she would have laughed at your poor taste. But as it is— believe me, it will not be her fault if her desire for revenge has not already been satisfied.

ADOLPH. I must know if it is so!

GUSTAV. Find out!

ADOLPH. Find out?

GUSTAV. Watch—I'll assist you, if you want me to.

ADOLPH. As I am to die anyhow— it may as well come first as last! What am I to do?

GUSTAV. First of all a piece of information: has your wife any vulnerable point?

ADOLPH. Hardly! I think she must have nine lives, like a cat.

GUSTAV. There—that was the boat whistling at the landing—now she'll soon be here.

ADOLPH. Then I must go down and meet her.

GUSTAV. No, you are to stay here. You have to be impolite. If her conscience is clear, you'll catch it until your ears tingle. If she is guilty, she'll come up and pet you.

ADOLPH. Are you so sure of that?

GUSTAV. Not quite, because a rabbit will sometimes turn and run in loops, but I'll follow. My room is nest to this. [He points to the door on the right] There I shall take up my position and watch you while you are playing the game in here. But when you are done, we'll change parts: I'll enter the cage and do tricks with the snake while you stick to the key-hole. Then we meet in the park to compare notes. But keep your back stiff. And if you feel yourself weakening, knock twice on the floor with a chair.

ADOLPH. All right!—But don't go away. I must be sure that you are in the next room.

GUSTAV. You can be quite sure of that. But don't get scared afterward, when you watch me dissecting a human soul and laying out its various parts on the table. They say it is rather hard on a beginner, but once you have seen it done, you never want to miss it.—And be sure to remember one thing: not a word about having met me, or having made any new acquaintance whatever while she was away. Not one word! And I'll discover her weak point by myself. Hush, she has arrived—she is in her room now. She's humming to herself. That means she is in a rage!—Now, straight in the back, please! And sit down on that chair over there, so that she has to sit here—then I can watch both of you at the same time.

ADOLPH. It's only fifteen minutes to dinner—and no new guests have arrived—for I haven't heard the bell ring. That means we shall be by ourselves—worse luck!

GUSTAV. Are you weak?

ADOLPH. I am nothing at all!—Yes, I am afraid of what is now coming! But I cannot keep it from coming! The stone has been set rolling—and it was not the first drop of water that started it— nor was it the last one—but all of them together.

GUSTAV. Let it roll then—for peace will come in no other way.

Good-bye for a while now! [Goes out]

(ADOLPH nods back at him. Until then he has been standing with the photograph in his hand. Now he tears it up and flings the pieces under the table. Then he sits down on a chair, pulls nervously at his tie, runs his fingers through his hair, crumples his coat lapel, and so on.)

TEKLA. [Enters, goes straight up to him and gives him a kiss; her manner is friendly, frank, happy, and engaging] Hello, little brother! How is he getting on?

ADOLPH. [Almost won over; speaking reluctantly and as if in jest] What mischief have you been up to now that makes you come and kiss me?

TEKLA. I'll tell you: I've spent an awful lot of money.

ADOLPH. You have had a good time then?

TEKLA. Very! But not exactly at that creche meeting. That was plain piffle, to tell the truth.—But what has little brother found to divert himself with while his Pussy was away?

(Her eyes wander around the room as if she were looking for somebody or sniffing something.)

ADOLPH. I've simply been bored.

TEKLA. And no company at all?

ADOLPH. Quite by myself.

TEKLA. [Watching him; she sits down on the sofa] Who has been sitting here? ADOLPH. Over there? Nobody.

TEKLA. That's funny! The seat is still warm, and there is a hollow here that looks as if it had been made by an elbow. Have you had lady callers?

ADOLPH. I? You don't believe it, do you?

TEKLA. But you blush. I think little brother is not telling the truth. Come and tell Pussy now what he has on his conscience.

(Draws him toward herself so that he sinks down with his head resting in her lap.)

ADOLPH. You're a little devil—do you know that?

TEKLA. No, I don't know anything at all about myself.

ADOLPH. You never think about yourself, do you?

TEKLA. [Sniffing and taking notes] I think of nothing but myself— I am a dreadful egoist. But what has made you turn so philosophical all at once?

ADOLPH. Put your hand on my forehead.

TEKLA. [Prattling as if to a baby] Has he got ants in his head again? Does he want me to take them away, does he? [Kisses him on the forehead] There now! Is it all right now?

ADOLPH. Now it's all right. [Pause]

TEKLA. Well, tell me now what you have been doing to make the time go? Have you painted anything?

ADOLPH. No, I am done with painting.

TEKLA. What? Done with painting?

ADOLPH. Yes, but don't scold me for it. How can I help it that I can't paint any longer!

TEKLA. What do you mean to do then?

ADOLPH. I'll become a sculptor.

TEKLA. What a lot of brand new ideas again!

ADOLPH. Yes, but please don't scold! Look at that figure over there.

TEKLA. [Uncovering the wax figure] Well, I declare!—Who is that meant for?

ADOLPH. Guess!

TEKLA. Is it Pussy? Has he got no shame at all?

ADOLPH. Is it like?

TEKLA. How can I tell when there is no face?

ADOLPH. Yes, but there is so much else—that's beautiful!

TEKLA. [Taps him playfully on the cheek] Now he must keep still or I'll have to kiss him.

ADOLPH. [Holding her back] Now, now!—Somebody might come!

TEKLA. Well, what do I care? Can't I kiss my own husband, perhaps? Oh yes, that's my lawful right.

ADOLPH. Yes, but don't you know—in the hotel here, they don't believe we are married, because we are kissing each other such a lot. And it makes no difference that we quarrel now and then, for lovers are said to do that also.

TEKLA. Well, but what's the use of quarrelling? Why can't he always be as nice as he is now? Tell me now? Can't he try? Doesn't he want us to be happy?

ADOLPH. Do I want it? Yes, but—

TEKLA. There we are again! Who has put it into his head that he is not to paint any longer?

ADOLPH. Who? You are always looking for somebody else behind me and my thoughts. Are you jealous?

TEKLA. Yes, I am. I'm afraid somebody might take him away from me.

ADOLPH. Are you really afraid of that? You who know that no other woman can take your place, and that I cannot live without you!

TEKLA. Well, I am not afraid of the women—it's your friends that fill your head with all sorts of notions.

ADOLPH. [Watching her] You are afraid then? Of what are you afraid?

TEKLA. [Getting up] Somebody has been here. Who has been here?

ADOLPH. Don't you wish me to look at you?

TEKLA. Not in that way: it's not the way you are accustomed to look at me.

ADOLPH. How was I looking at you

then?

TEKLA. Way up under my eyelids.

ADOLPH. Under your eyelids—yes, I wanted to see what is behind them.

TEKLA. See all you can! There is nothing that needs to be hidden. But—you talk differently, too—you use expressions—[studying him] you philosophise—that's what you do! [Approaches him threateningly] Who has been here?

ADOLPH. Nobody but my physician.

TEKLA. Your physician? Who is he?

ADOLPH. That doctor from Stromstad.

TEKLA. What's his name?

ADOLPH. Sjoberg.

TEKLA. What did he have to say?

ADOLPH. He said—well—among other things he said—that I am on the verge of epilepsy—

TEKLA. Among other things? What more did he say?

ADOLPH. Something very unpleasant.

TEKLA. Tell me!

ADOLPH. He forbade us to live as man and wife for a while.

TEKLA. Oh, that's it! Didn't I just guess it! They want to separate us! That's what I have understood a long time!

ADOLPH. You can't have understood, because there was nothing to understand.

TEKLA. Oh yes, I have!

ADOLPH. How can you see what doesn't exist, unless your fear of something has stirred up your fancy into seeing what has never existed? What is it you fear? That I might borrow somebody else's eyes in order to see you as you are, and not as you seem to be?

TEKLA. Keep your imagination in check, Adolph! It is the beast that dwells in man's soul.

ADOLPH. Where did you learn that? From those chaste young men on the boat—did you?

TEKLA. [Not at all abashed] Yes, there is something to be learned from youth also.

ADOLPH. I think you are already beginning to have a taste for youth?

TEKLA. I have always liked youth. That's why I love you. Do you object?

ADOLPH. No, but I should prefer to have no partners.

TEKLA. [Prattling roguishly] My heart is so big, little brother, that there is room in it for many more than him.

ADOLPH. But little brother doesn't want any more brothers.

TEKLA. Come here to Pussy now and get his hair pulled because he is jealous—no, envious is the right word for it!

(Two knocks with a chair are heard from the adjoining room, where GUSTAV is.)

ADOLPH. No, I don't want to play now. I want to talk seriously.

TEKLA. [Prattling] Mercy me, does he want to talk seriously? Dreadful, how serious he's become! [Takes hold of his head and kisses him] Smile a little—there now!

ADOLPH. [Smiling against his will] Oh, you're the—I might almost think you knew how to use magic!

TEKLA. Well, can't he see now? That's why he shouldn't start any trouble—or I might use my magic to make him invisible!

ADOLPH. [Gets up] Will you sit for me a moment, Tekla? With the side of your face this way, so that I can put a face on my figure.

TEKLA. Of course, I will.

[Turns her head so he can see her in profile.]

ADOLPH. [Gazes hard at her while pretending to work at the figure] Don't think of me now—but of somebody else.

TEKLA. I'll think of my latest conquest.

ADOLPH. That chaste young man?

TEKLA. Exactly! He had a pair of the prettiest, sweetest moustaches, and his cheek looked like a peach—it was so soft and rosy that you just wanted to bite it.

ADOLPH. [Darkening] Please keep that expression about the mouth.

TEKLA. What expression?

ADOLPH. A cynical, brazen one that I have never seen before.

TEKLA. [Making a face] This one?

ADOLPH. Just that one! [Getting up] Do you know how Bret Harte pictures an adulteress?

TEKLA. [Smiling] No, I have never read Bret Something.

ADOLPH. As a pale creature that cannot blush.

TEKLA. Not at all? But when she meets her lover, then she must blush, I am sure, although her husband or Mr. Bret may not be allowed to see it.

ADOLPH. Are you so sure of that?

TEKLA. [As before] Of course, as the husband is not capable of bringing the blood up to her head, he cannot hope to behold the charming spectacle.

ADOLPH. [Enraged] Tekla!

TEKLA. Oh, you little ninny!

ADOLPH. Tekla!

TEKLA. He should call her Pussy—then I might get up a pretty little blush for his sake. Does he want me to?

ADOLPH. [Disarmed] You minx, I'm so angry with you, that I could bite you!

TEKLA. [Playfully] Come and bite me then!—Come!

[Opens her arms to him.]

ADOLPH. [Puts his hands around her neck and kisses her] Yes, I'll bite you to death!

TEKLA. [Teasingly] Look out—somebody might come!

ADOLPH. Well, what do I care! I care for nothing else in the world if I can only have you!

TEKLA. And when, you don't have me any longer?

ADOLPH. Then I shall die!

TEKLA. But you are not afraid of losing me, are you—as I am too old to be wanted by anybody else?

ADOLPH. You have not forgotten my words yet, Tekla! I take it all back now!

TEKLA. Can you explain to me why you are at once so jealous and so cocksure?

ADOLPH. No, I cannot explain anything at all. But it's possible that the thought of somebody else having possessed you may still be gnawing within me. At times it appears to me as if our love were nothing but a fiction, an attempt at self-defence, a passion kept up as a matter of honor—and I can't think of anything that would give me more pain than to have HIM know that I am unhappy. Oh, I have never seen him—but the mere thought that a person exists who is waiting for my misfortune to arrive, who is daily calling down curses on my head, who will roar with laughter when I perish—the mere idea of it obsesses me, drives me nearer to you, fascinates me, paralyses me!

TEKLA. Do you think I would let him have that joy? Do you think I would make his prophecy come true?

ADOLPH. No, I cannot think you would.

TEKLA. Why don't you keep calm then?

ADOLPH. No, you upset me constantly by your coquetry. Why do you play that kind of game?

TEKLA. It is no game. I want to be admired—that's all!

ADOLPH. Yes, but only by men!

TEKLA. Of course! For a woman is never admired by other women.

ADOLPH. Tell me, have you heard anything—from him—recently?

TEKLA. Not in the last six months.

ADOLPH. Do you ever think of him?

TEKLA. No!—Since the child died we have broken off our correspondence.

ADOLPH. And you have never seen him at all?

TEKLA. No, I understand he is living somewhere down on the West Coast. But why is all this coming into your head just now?

ADOLPH. I don't know. But during the last few days, while I was alone, I kept thinking of him—how he might have felt when he was left alone that time.

TEKLA. Are you having an attack of bad conscience?

ADOLPH. I am.

TEKLA. You feel like a thief, do you?

ADOLPH. Almost!

TEKLA. Isn't that lovely! Women can be stolen as you steal children or chickens? And you regard me as his chattel or personal property. I am very much obliged to you!

ADOLPH. No, I regard you as his wife. And that's a good deal more than property—for there can be no substitute. TEKLA. Oh, yes! If you only heard that he had married again, all these foolish notions would leave you.—Have you not taken his place with me?

ADOLPH. Well, have I?—And did you ever love him?

TEKLA. Of course, I did!

ADOLPH. And then—

TEKLA. I grew tired of him!

ADOLPH. And if you should tire of me also?

TEKLA. But I won't!

ADOLPH. If somebody else should turn up—one who had all the qualities you are looking for in a man now—suppose only—then you would leave me?

TEKLA. No.

ADOLPH. If he captivated you? So that you couldn't live without him? Then you would leave me, of course?

TEKLA. No, that doesn't follow.

ADOLPH. But you couldn't love two at the same time, could you?

TEKLA. Yes! Why not?

ADOLPH. That's something I cannot understand.

TEKLA. But things exist although you do not understand them. All persons are not made in the same way, you know.

ADOLPH. I begin to see now!

TEKLA. No, really!

ADOLPH. No, really? [A pause follows, during which he seems to struggle with some—memory that will not come back] Do you know, Tekla, that your frankness is beginning to be painful?

TEKLA. And yet it used to be my foremost virtue In your mind, and one that you taught me.

ADOLPH. Yes, but it seems to me as if you were hiding something behind that frankness of yours.

TEKLA. That's the new tactics, you know.

ADOLPH. I don't know why, but this place has suddenly become offensive to me. If you feel like it, we might return home—this evening!

TEKLA. What kind of notion is that? I have barely arrived and I don't feel like starting on another trip.

ADOLPH. But I want to.

TEKLA. Well, what's that to me?—You can go!

ADOLPH. But I demand that you take the next boat with me!

TEKLA. Demand?—What are you talking about?

ADOLPH. Do you realise that you are my wife?

TEKLA. Do you realise that you are my husband?

ADOLPH. Well, there's a difference between those two things.

TEKLA. Oh, that's the way you are talking now!—You have never loved me!

ADOLPH. Haven't I?

TEKLA. No, for to love is to give.

ADOLPH. To love like a man is to give; to love like a woman is to take.—And I have given, given, given!

TEKLA. Pooh! What have you given?

ADOLPH. Everything!

TEKLA. That's a lot! And if it be true, then I must have taken it. Are you beginning to send in bills for your gifts now? And if I have taken anything, this proves only my love for you. A woman cannot receive anything except from her lover

ADOLPH. Her lover, yes! There you spoke the truth! I have been your lover, but never your husband.

TEKLA. Well, isn't that much more agreeable—to escape playing chaperon? But if you are not satisfied with your position, I'll send you packing, for I don't want a husband.

ADOLPH. No, that's what I have noticed. For a while ago, when you began to sneak away from me like a thief with his booty, and when you began to seek company of your own where you could flaunt my plumes and display my gems, then I felt, like reminding you of your debt. And at once I became a troublesome creditor whom you wanted to get rid of. You wanted to repudiate your own notes, and in order not to increase your debt to me, you stopped pillaging my safe and began to try those of other people instead. Without having done anything myself, I became to you merely the husband. And now I am going to be your husband whether you like it or not, as I am not allowed to be your lover any longer,

TEKLA. [Playfully] Now he shouldn't talk nonsense, the sweet little idiot!

ADOLPH. Look out: it's dangerous to think everybody an idiot but oneself!

TEKLA. But that's what everybody thinks.

ADOLPH. And I am beginning to suspect that he—your former husband—was not so much of an idiot after all.

TEKLA. Heavens! Are you beginning to sympathise with—him?

ADOLPH. Yes, not far from it,

TEKLA. Well, well! Perhaps you would like to make his acquaintance and pour out your overflowing heart to him? What a striking picture! But I am also beginning to feel drawn to him, as I am growing more and more tired of acting as wetnurse. For he was at least a man, even though he had the fault of being married to me.

ADOLPH. There, you see! But you had better not talk so loud—we might be overheard.

TEKLA. What would it matter if they took us for married people?

ADOLPH. So now you are getting fond of real male men also, and at the same time you have a taste for chaste young men?

TEKLA. There are no limits to what I can like, as you may see. My heart is open to everybody and everything, to the big and the small, the handsome and the ugly, the new and the old—I love the whole world.

ADOLPH. Do you know what that means?

TEKLA. No, I don't know anything at all. I just FEEL.

ADOLPH. It means that old age is near.

TEKLA. There you are again! Take care!

ADOLPH. Take care yourself!

TEKLA. Of what?

ADOLPH. Of the knife!

TEKLA. [Prattling] Little brother had better not play with such dangerous things.

ADOLPH. I have quit playing.

TEKLA. Oh, it's earnest, is it? Dead earnest! Then I'll show you that—you are mistaken. That is to say—you'll never see it, never know it, but all the rest of the world will know It. And you'll suspect it, you'll believe it, and you'll never have another moment's peace. You'll have the feeling of being ridiculous, of being deceived, but you'll never get any proof of it. For that's what married men never get.

ADOLPH. You hate me then?

TEKLA. No, I don't. And I don't think I shall either. But that's probably because you are nothing to me but a child.

ADOLPH. At this moment, yes. But do you remember how it was while the storm swept over us? Then you lay there like an infant in arms and just cried. Then you had to sit on my lap, and I had to kiss your eyes to sleep. Then I had to be your nurse; had to see that you fixed your hair before going out; had to send your shoes to the cobbler, and see that there was food in the house. I had to sit by your side, holding your hand for hours at a time: you were afraid, afraid of the whole world, because you didn't have a single friend, and because you were crushed by the hostility of public opinion. I had to talk courage into you until my mouth was dry and my head ached. I had to make myself believe that I was strong. I had to force myself into believing in the future. And so I brought you back to life, when you seemed already dead. Then you admired me. Then I was the man—not that kind of athlete you had just left, but the man of willpower, the mesmerist who instilled new nervous energy into your flabby muscles and charged your empty brain with a new store of electricity. And then I gave you back your reputation. I brought you new friends, furnished you with a little court of people who, for the sake of friendship to me, let themselves be lured into admiring you. I set you to rule me and my house. Then I painted my best pictures, glimmering with reds and blues on backgrounds of gold, and there was not an exhibition then where I didn't hold a place of honour. Sometimes you were St. Cecilia, and sometimes Mary Stuart—or little Karin, whom King Eric loved. And I turned public attention in your direction. I compelled the clamorous herd to see yon with my own infatuated vision. I plagued them with your personality, forced you literally down their throats, until that sympathy which makes everything possible became yours at last—and you could stand on your own feet. When you reached that far, then my strength was used up, and I collapsed from the overstrain—in lifting you up, I had pushed myself down. I was taken ill, and my illness seemed an annoyance to you at the moment when all life had just begun to smile at you- -and sometimes it seemed to me as if, in your heart, there was a secret desire to get rid of your creditor and the witness of your rise. Your love began to change into that of a grown-up sister, and for lack of better I accustomed myself to the new part of little brother. Your tenderness for me remained, and even increased, but it was mingled with a suggestion of pity that had in it a good deal of contempt. And this changed into open scorn as my talent withered and your own sun rose higher. But in some mysterious way the fountainhead of your inspiration seemed to dry up when I could no longer replenish it—or rather when you wanted to show its independence of me. And at last both of us began to lose ground. And then you looked for somebody to put the blame on. A new victim! For you are weak, and you can never carry your own burdens of guilt and debt. And so you picked me for a scapegoat and doomed me to slaughter. But when you cut my thews, you didn't realise that you were also crippling yourself, for by this time our years of common life had made twins of us. You were a shoot sprung from my stem, and you wanted to cut yourself loose before the shoot had put out roots of its own, and that's why you couldn't grow by yourself. And my stem could not spare its main branch—and so stem and branch must die together.

TEKLA. What you mean with all this, of course, is that you have written my books.

ADOLPH. No, that's what you want me to mean in order to make me out a liar. I don't use such crude expressions as you do, and I spoke for something like five minutes to get in all the nuances, all the halftones, all the transitions—but your hand-organ has only a single note in it.

TEKLA. Yes, but the summary of the whole story is that you have written my books.

ADOLPH. No, there is no summary. You cannot reduce a chord into a single note. You cannot translate a varied life into a sum of one figure. I have made no blunt statements like that of having written your books.

TEKLA. But that's what you meant!

ADOLPH. [Beyond himself] I did not mean it.

TEKLA. But the sum of it—

ADOLPH. [Wildly] There can be no sum without an addition. You get an endless decimal fraction for quotient when your division does not work out evenly. I have not added anything.

TEKLA. But I can do the adding myself.

ADOLPH. I believe it, but then I am not doing it.

TEKLA. No, but that's what you wanted to do.

ADOLPH. [Exhausted, closing his eyes] No, no, no—don't speak to me—you'll drive me into convulsions. Keep silent! Leave me alone! You mutilate my brain with your clumsy pincers—you put your claws into my thoughts and tear them to pieces!

(He seems almost unconscious and sits staring straight ahead while his thumbs are bent inward against the palms of his hands.)

TEKLA. [Tenderly] What is it? Are you sick?

(ADOLPH motions her away.)

TEKLA. Adolph!

(ADOLPH shakes his head at her.)

TEKLA. Adolph.

ADOLPH. Yes.

TEKLA. Do you admit that you were unjust a moment ago?

ADOLPH. Yes, yes, yes, yes, I admit!

TEKLA. And do you ask my pardon?

ADOLPH. Yes, yes, yes, I ask your pardon—if you only won't speak to me!

TEKLA. Kiss my hand then!

ADOLPH. [Kissing her hand] I'll kiss your hand—if you only don't speak to me!

TEKLA. And now you had better go out for a breath of fresh air before dinner.

ADOLPH. Yes, I think I need it. And then we'll pack and leave.

TEKLA. No!

ADOLPH. [On his feet] Why? There must be a reason.

TEKLA. The reason is that I have promised to be at the concert to-night.

ADOLPH. Oh, that's it!

TEKLA. Yes, that's it. I have promised to attend—

ADOLPH. Promised? Probably you said only that you might go, and that wouldn't prevent you from saying now that you won't go.

TEKLA. No, I am not like you: I keep my word.

ADOLPH. Of course, promises should be kept, but we don't have to live up to every little word we happen to drop. Perhaps there is somebody who has made you promise to go.

TEKLA. Yes.

ADOLPH. Then you can ask to be released from your promise because your husband is sick.

TEKLA. No, I don't want to do that, and you are not sick enough to be kept from going with me.

ADOLPH. Why do you always want to drag me along? Do you feel safer then?

TEKLA. I don't know what you mean.

ADOLPH. That's what you always say when you know I mean something that—doesn't please you.

TEKLA. So-o! What is it now that doesn't please me?

ADOLPH. Oh, I beg you, don't begin over again—Good-bye for a while!

(Goes out through the door in the rear and then turns to the right.)

(TEKLA is left alone. A moment later GUSTAV enters and goes straight up to the table as if looking for a newspaper. He pretends not to see TEKLA.)

TEKLA. [Shows agitation, but manages to control herself] Oh, is it you?

GUSTAV. Yes, it's me—I beg your pardon!

TEKLA. Which way did you come?

GUSTAV. By land. But—I am not going to stay, as—

TEKLA. Oh, there is no reason why you shouldn't.—Well, it was some time ago—

GUSTAV. Yes, some time.

TEKLA. You have changed a great deal.

GUSTAV. And you are as charming as ever. A little younger, if anything. Excuse me, however—I am not going to spoil your happiness by my presence. And if I had known you were here, I should never—

TEKLA. If you don't think it improper, I should like you to stay.

GUSTAV. On my part there could be no objection, but I fear—well, whatever I say, I am sure to offend you.

TEKLA. Sit down a moment. You don't offend me, for you possess that rare gift—which was always yours—of tact and politeness.

GUSTAV. It's very kind of you. But one could hardly expect—that your husband might regard my qualities in the same generous light as you.

TEKLA. On the contrary, he has just been speaking of you in very sympathetic terms.

GUSTAV. Oh!—Well, everything becomes covered up by time, like names cut in a tree—and not even dislike can maintain itself permanently in our minds.

TEKLA. He has never disliked you, for he has never seen you. And as for me, I have always cherished a dream—that of seeing you come together as friends—or at least of seeing you meet for once in my presence—of seeing you shake hands—and then go your different ways again.

GUSTAV. It has also been my secret longing to see her whom I used to love more than my own life—to make sure that she was in good hands. And although I have heard nothing but good of him, and am familiar with all his work,

I should nevertheless have liked, before it grew too late, to look into his eyes and beg him to take good care of the treasure Providence has placed in his possession. In that way I hoped also to lay the hatred that must have developed instinctively between us; I wished to bring some peace and humility into my soul, so that I might manage to live through the rest of my sorrowful days.

TEKLA. You have uttered my own thoughts, and you have understood me. I thank you for it!

GUSTAV. Oh, I am a man of small account, and have always been too insignificant to keep you in the shadow. My monotonous way of living, my drudgery, my narrow horizons—all that could not satisfy a soul like yours, longing for liberty. I admit it. But you understand—you who have searched the human soul—what it cost me to make such a confession to myself.

TEKLA. It is noble, it is splendid, to acknowledge one's own shortcomings—and it's not everybody that's capable of it. [Sighs] But yours has always been an honest, and faithful, and reliable nature—one that I had to respect—but—

GUSTAV. Not always—not at that time! But suffering purifies, sorrow ennobles, and—I have suffered!

TEKLA. Poor Gustav! Can you forgive me? Tell me, can you?

GUSTAV. Forgive? What? I am the one who must ask you to forgive.

TEKLA. [Changing tone] I believe we are crying, both of us—we who are old enough to know better!

GUSTAV. [Feeling his way] Old? Yes, I am old. But you—you grow younger every day.

(He has by that time manoeuvred himself up to the chair on the left and sits down on it, whereupon TEKLA sits down on the sofa.)

TEKLA. Do you think so?

GUSTAV. And then you know how to dress.

TEKLA. I learned that from you. Don't you remember how you figured out what colors would be most becoming to me?

GUSTAV. No.

TEKLA. Yes, don't you remember—hm!—I can even recall how you used to be angry with me whenever I failed to have at least a touch of crimson about my dress.

GUSTAV. No, not angry! I was never angry with you.

TEKLA. Oh, yes, when you wanted to teach me how to think—do you remember? For that was something I couldn't do at all.

GUSTAV. Of course, you could. It's something every human being does. And you have become quite keen at it—at least when you write.

TEKLA. [Unpleasantly impressed; hurrying her words] Well, my dear Gustav, it is pleasant to see you anyhow, and especially in a peaceful way like this.

GUSTAV. Well, I can hardly be called a troublemaker, and you had a pretty peaceful time with me.

TEKLA. Perhaps too much so.

GUSTAV. Oh! But you see, I thought you wanted me that way. It was at least the impression you gave me while we were engaged.

TEKLA. Do you think one really knows what one wants at that time? And then the mammas insist on all kinds of pretensions, of course.

GUSTAV. Well, now you must be having all the excitement you can wish. They say that life among artists is rather swift, and I don't think your husband can be called a sluggard.

TEKLA. You can get too much of a good thing.

GUSTAV. [Trying a new tack] What! I do believe you are still wearing the ear-rings I gave you?

TEKLA. [Embarrassed] Why not? There was never any quarrel between us—and then I thought I might wear them as a token—and a reminder—that we were not enemies. And then, you know, it is impossible to buy this kind of ear-rings any longer. [Takes off one of her ear-rings.]

GUSTAV. Oh, that's all right, but what does your husband say of it?

TEKLA. Why should I mind what he says?

GUSTAV. Don't you mind that?—But you may be doing him an injury. It is likely to make him ridiculous.

TEKLA. [Brusquely, as if speaking to herself almost] He was that before!

GUSTAV. [Rises when he notes her difficulty in putting back the ear-ring] May I help you, perhaps?

TEKLA. Oh—thank you!

GUSTAV. [Pinching her ear] That tiny ear!—Think only if your husband could see us now!

TEKLA. Wouldn't he howl, though!

GUSTAV. Is he jealous also?

TEKLA. Is he? I should say so!

[A noise is heard from the room on the right.]

GUSTAV. Who lives in that room?

TEKLA. I don't know.—But tell me how you are getting along and what you are doing?

GUSTAV. Tell me rather how you are getting along?

(TEKLA is visibly confused, and without realising what she is doing, she takes the cover off the wax figure.)

GUSTAV. Hello! What's that?—Well!—It must be you!

TEKLA. I don't believe so.

GUSTAV. But it is very like you.

TEKLA. [Cynically] Do you think so?

GUSTAV. That reminds me of the story—you know it—"How could your majesty see that?"

TEKLA, [Laughing aloud] You are impossible!—Do you know any new stories?

GUSTAV. No, but you ought to have some.

TEKLA. Oh, I never hear anything funny nowadays.

GUSTAV. Is he modest also?

TEKLA. Oh—well—

GUSTAV. Not an everything?

TEKLA. He isn't well just now.

GUSTAV. Well, why should little brother put his nose into other people's hives?

TEKLA. [Laughing] You crazy thing!

GUSTAV. Poor chap!—Do you remember once when we were just married—we lived in this very room. It was furnished differently in those days. There was a chest of drawers against that wall there—and over there stood the big bed.

TEKLA. Now you stop!

GUSTAV. Look at me!

TEKLA. Well, why shouldn't I? [They look hard at each other.]

GUSTAV. Do you think a person can ever forget anything that has made a very deep impression on him?

TEKLA. No! And our memories have a tremendous power. Particularly the memories of our youth.

GUSTAV. Do you remember when I first met you? Then you were a pretty little girl: a slate on which parents and governesses had made a few scrawls that I had to wipe out. And then I filled it with inscriptions that suited my own mind, until you believed the slate could hold nothing more. That's the reason, you know, why I shouldn't care to be in your husband's place—well, that's his business! But it's also the reason why I take pleasure in meeting you again. Our thoughts fit together exactly. And as I sit here and chat with you, it seems to me like drinking old wine of my own bottling. Yes, it's my own wine, but it has gained a great deal in flavour! And now, when I am about to marry again, I have purposely picked out a young girl whom I can educate to suit myself. For the woman, you know, is the man's child, and if she is not, he becomes hers, and then the world turns topsy-turvy.

TEKLA. Are you going to marry again?

GUSTAV. Yes, I want to try my luck once more, but this time I am going to make a better start, so that it won't end again with a spill.

TEKLA. Is she good looking?

GUSTAV. Yes, to me. But perhaps I am too old. It's queer—now when chance has brought me together with you again—I am beginning to doubt whether it will be possible to play the game over again.

TEKLA. How do you mean?

GUSTAV. I can feel that my roots stick in your soil, and the old wounds are beginning to break open. You are a dangerous woman, Tekla!

TEKLA. Am I? And my young husband says that I can make no more conquests.

GUSTAV. That means he has ceased to love you.

TEKLA. Well, I can't quite make out what love means to him.

GUSTAV. You have been playing hide and seek so long that at last you cannot find each other at all. Such things do happen. You have had to play the innocent to yourself, until he has lost his courage. There ARE some drawbacks to a change, I tell you—there are drawbacks to it, indeed.

TEKLA. Do you mean to reproach—

GUSTAV. Not at all! Whatever happens is to a certain extent necessary, for if it didn't happen, something else would—but now it did happen, and so it had to happen.

TEKLA. YOU are a man of discernment. And I have never met anybody with whom I liked so much to exchange ideas. You are so utterly free from all morality and preaching, and you ask so little of people, that it is possible to be oneself in your presence. Do you know, I am jealous of your intended wife!

GUSTAV. And do you realise that I am jealous of your husband?

TEKLA. [Rising] And now we must part! Forever!

GUSTAV. Yes, we must part! But not without a farewell—or what do you say?

TEKLA. [Agitated] No!

GUSTAV. [Following after her] Yes!—Let us have a farewell! Let us drown our memories—you know, there are intoxications so deep that when you wake up all memories are gone. [Putting his arm around her waist] You have been dragged down by a diseased spirit, who is infecting you with his own anaemia. I'll breathe new life into you. I'll make your talent blossom again in your autumn days, like a remontant rose. I'll——

(Two LADIES in travelling dress are seen in the doorway leading to the veranda. They look surprised. Then they point at those within, laugh, and disappear.)

TEKLA. [Freeing herself] Who was that?

GUSTAV. [Indifferently] Some tourists.

TEKLA. Leave me alone! I am afraid of you!

GUSTAV. Why?

TEKLA. You take my soul away from me!

GUSTAV. And give you my own in its place! And you have no soul for that matter—it's nothing but a delusion.

TEKLA. You have a way of saying impolite things so that nobody can be angry with you.

GUSTAV. It's because you feel that I hold the first mortgage on you—Tell me now, when—and—where?

TEKLA. No, it wouldn't be right to him. I think he is still in love with me, and I don't want to do any more harm.

GUSTAV. He does not love you! Do you want proofs?

TEKLA. Where can you get them?

GUSTAV. [Picking up the pieces of the photograph from the floor] Here! See for yourself!

TEKLA. Oh, that's an outrage!

GUSTAV. Do you see? Now then, where? And where?

TEKLA. The false-hearted wretch!

GUSTAV. When?

TEKLA. He leaves to-night, with the eight-o'clock boat.

GUSTAV. And then—

TEKLA. At nine! [A noise is heard from the adjoining room] Who can be living in there that makes such a racket?

GUSTAV. Let's see! [Goes over and looks through the keyhole] There's a table that has been upset, and a smashed water caraffe— that's all! I shouldn't wonder if they had left a dog locked up in there.—At nine o'clock then?

TEKLA. All right! And let him answer for it himself.—What a depth of deceit! And he who has always preached about truthfulness, and tried to teach me to tell the truth!—But wait a little—how was it now? He received me with something like hostility—didn't meet me at the landing—and then—and then he made some remark about young men on board the boat, which I pretended not to hear—but how could he know? Wait—and then he began to philosophise about women—and then the spectre of you seemed to be haunting him—and he talked of becoming a sculptor, that being the art of the time—exactly in accordance with your old speculations!

GUSTAV. No, really!

TEKLA. No, really?—Oh, now I understand! Now I begin to see what a hideous creature you are! You have been here before and stabbed him to death! It was you who had been sitting there on the sofa; it was you who made him think himself an epileptic—that he had to live in celibacy; that he ought to rise in rebellion against his wife; yes, it was you!—How long have you been here?

GUSTAV. I have been here a week.

TEKLA. It was you, then, I saw on board the boat?

GUSTAV. It was.

TEKLA. And now you were thinking you could trap me?

GUSTAV. It has been done.

TEKLA. Not yet!

GUSTAV. Yes!

TEKLA. Like a wolf you went after my lamb. You came here with a villainous plan to break up my happiness, and you were carrying it out, when my eyes were opened, and I foiled you.

GUSTAV. Not quite that way, if you please. This is how it happened in reality. Of course, it has been my secret hope that disaster might overtake you. But I felt practically certain that no interference on my part was required. And besides, I have been far too busy to have any time left for intriguing. But when I happened to be moving about a bit, and happened to see you with those young men on board the boat, then I guessed the time had come for me to take a look at the situation. I came here, and your lamb threw itself into the arms of the wolf. I won his affection by some sort of reminiscent impression which I shall not be tactless enough to explain to you. At first he aroused my sympathy, because he seemed to be in the same fix as I was once. But then he happened to touch old wounds—that book, you know, and "the idiot"—and I was seized with a wish to pick him to pieces, and to mix up these so thoroughly that they couldn't be put together again—and I succeeded, thanks to the painstaking way in which you had done the work of preparation. Then I had to deal with you. For you were the spring that had kept the works moving, and you had to be taken apart—and what a buzzing followed!—When I came in here, I didn't know exactly what to say. Like a chess-player, I had laid a number of tentative plans, of course, but my play had to depend on your moves. One thing led to the other, chance lent me a hand, and finally I had you where I wanted you.—Now you are caught!

TEKLA. No!

GUSTAV. Yes, you are! What you least wanted has happened. The world at large, represented by two lady tourists—whom I had not sent for, as I am not an intriguer—the world has seen how you became reconciled to your former husband, and how you sneaked back repentantly into his faithful arms. Isn't that enough?

TEKLA. It ought to be enough for your revenge—But tell me, how can you, who are so enlightened and so right-minded—how is it possible that you, who think whatever happens must happen, and that all our actions are determined in advance—

GUSTAV. [Correcting her] To a certain extent determined.

TEKLA. That's the same thing!

GUSTAV. No!

TEKLA. [Disregarding him] How is it possible that you, who hold me guiltless, as I was driven by my nature and the circumstances into acting as I did—how can you think yourself entitled to revenge—?

GUSTAV. For that very reason—for the reason that my nature and the circumstances drove me into seeking revenge. Isn't that giving both sides a square deal? But do you know why you two had to get the worst of it in this struggle?

(TEKLA looks scornful.)

GUSTAV. And why you were doomed to be fooled? Because I am stronger than you, and wiser also. You have been the idiot—and he! And now you may perceive that a man need not be an idiot because he doesn't write novels or paint pictures. It might be well for you to bear this in mind.

TEKLA. Are you then entirely without feelings?

GUSTAV. Entirely! And for that very reason, you know, I am capable of thinking—in which you have had no experience whatever-and of acting—in which you have just had some slight experience.

TEKLA. And all this merely because I have hurt your vanity?

GUSTAV. Don't call that MERELY! You had better not go around hurting other people's vanity. They have no more sensitive spot than that.

TEKLA. Vindictive wretch—shame on you!

GUSTAV. Dissolute wretch—shame on you!

TEKLA. Oh, that's my character, is it?

GUSTAV. Oh, that's my character, is it?—You ought to learn something about human nature in others before you give your own nature free rein. Otherwise you may get hurt, and then there will be wailing and gnashing of teeth.

TEKLA. You can never forgive:—

GUSTAV. Yes, I have forgiven you!

TEKLA. You!

GUSTAV. Of course! Have I raised a hand against you during all these years? No! And now I came here only to have a look at you, and it was enough to burst your bubble. Have I uttered a single reproach? Have I moralised or preached sermons? No! I played a joke or two on your dear consort, and nothing more was needed to finish him.—But there is no reason why I, the complainant, should be defending myself as I am now—Tekla! Have you nothing at all to reproach yourself with?

TEKLA. Nothing at all! Christians say that our actions are governed by Providence; others call it Fate; in either case, are we not free from all liability?

GUSTAV. In a measure, yes; but there is always a narrow margin left unprotected, and there the liability applies in spite of all. And sooner or later the creditors make their appearance. Guiltless, but accountable! Guiltless in regard to one who is no more; accountable to oneself and one's fellow beings.

TEKLA. So you came here to dun me?

GUSTAV. I came to take back what you had stolen, not what you had received as a gift. You had stolen my honour, and I could recover it only by taking yours. This, I think, was my right—or was it not?

TEKLA. Honour? Hm! And now you feel satisfied?

GUSTAV. Now I feel satisfied. [Rings for a waiter.]

TEKLA. And now you are going home to your fiancee?

GUSTAV. I have no fiancee! Nor am I ever going to have one. I am not going home, for I have no home, and don't want one.

(A WAITER comes in.)

GUSTAV. Get me my bill—I am leaving by the eight o'clock boat.

(THE WAITER bows and goes out.)

TEKLA. Without making up?

GUSTAV. Making up? You use such a lot of words that have lost their— meaning. Why should we make up? Perhaps you want all three of us to live together? You, if anybody, ought to make up by making good what you took away, but this you cannot do. You just took, and what you took you consumed, so that there is nothing left to restore. —Will it satisfy you if I say like this: forgive me that you tore my heart to pieces; forgive me that you disgraced me; forgive me that you made me the laughing-stock of my pupils through every week-day of seven long years; forgive me that I set you free from parental restraints, that I released you from the tyranny of ignorance and superstition, that I set you to rule my house, that I gave you position and friends, that I made a woman out of the child you were before? Forgive me as I forgive you!— Now I have torn up your note! Now you can go and settle your account with the other one!

TEKLA. What have you done with him? I am beginning to suspect— something terrible!

GUSTAV. With him? Do you still love him?

TEKLA. Yes!

GUSTAV. And a moment ago it was me! Was that also true?

TEKLA. It was true.

GUSTAV. Do you know what you are then?

TEKLA. You despise me?

GUSTAV. I pity you. It is a trait—I don't call it a fault—just a trait, which is rendered disadvantageous by its results. Poor Tekla! I don't know—but it seems almost as if I were feeling a certain regret, although I am as free from any guilt—as you! But perhaps it will be useful to you to feel what I felt that time.— Do you know where your husband is?

TEKLA. I think I know now—he is in that room in there! And he has heard everything! And seen everything! And the man who sees his own wraith dies!

(ADOLPH appears in the doorway leading to the veranda. His face is white as a sheet, and there is a bleeding scratch on one cheek. His eyes are staring and void of all expression. His lips are covered with froth.)

GUSTAV. [Shrinking back] No, there he is!—Now you can settle with him and see if he proves as generous as I have been.—Good-bye!

(He goes toward the left, but stops before he reaches the door.)

TEKLA. [Goes to meet ADOLPH with open arms] Adolph!

(ADOLPH leans against the doorjamb and sinks gradually to the floor.)

TEKLA. [Throwing herself upon his prostrate body and caressing him] Adolph! My own child! Are you still alive—oh, speak, speak!- -Please forgive your nasty Tekla! Forgive me, forgive me, forgive me!—Little brother must say something, I tell him!—No, good God, he doesn't hear! He is dead! O God in heaven! O my God! Help!

GUSTAV. Why, she really must have loved HIM, too!—Poor creature!

(Curtain.)

PARIAH

INTRODUCTION

Both "Creditors" and "Pariah" were written in the winter of 1888- 89 at Holte, near Copenhagen, where Strindberg, assisted by his first wife, was then engaged in starting what he called a "Scandinavian Experimental Theatre." In March, 1889, the two plays were given by students from the University of Copenhagen, and with Mrs. von Essen Strindberg as Tekla. A couple of weeks later the performance was repeated across the Sound, in the Swedish city of Malmo, on which occasion the writer of this introduction, then a young actor, assisted in the stage management. One of the actors was Gustav Wied, a Danish playwright and novelist, whose exquisite art since then has won him European fame. In the audience was Ola Hansson, a Swedish novelist and poet who had just published a short story from which Strindberg, according to his own acknowledgment on playbill and title-page, had taken the name and the theme of "Pariah."

Mr. Hansson has printed a number of letters (Tilskueren, Copenhagen, July, 1912) written to him by Strindberg about that time, as well as some very informative comments of his own. Concerning the performance of Malmo he writes: "It gave me a very unpleasant sensation. What did it mean? Why had Strindberg turned my simple theme upsidedown so that it became unrecognisable? Not a vestige of the 'theme from Ola Hansson' remained. Yet he had even suggested that he and I act the play together, I not knowing that it was to be a duel between two criminals. And he had at first planned to call it 'Aryan and Pariah'—which meant, of course, that the strong Aryan, Strindberg was to crush the weak Pariah, Hansson, coram populo."

In regard to his own story Mr. Hansson informs us that it dealt with "a man who commits a forgery and then tells about it, doing both in a sort of somnambulistic state whereby everything is left vague and undefined." At that moment "Raskolnikov" was in the air, so to speak. And without wanting in any way to suggest imitation, I feel sure that the groundnote of the story was distinctly Dostoievskian. Strindberg himself had been reading Nietzsche and was— largely under the pressure of a reaction against the popular disapproval of his anti-feministic attitude—being driven more and more into a superman philosophy which reached its climax in the two novels "Chandalah" (1889) and "At the Edge of the Sea" (1890). The Nietzschean note is unmistakable in the two plays contained in the present volume.

But these plays are strongly colored by something else—by something that is neither Hansson-Dostoievski nor Strindberg-Nietzsche. The solution of the problem is found in the letters published by Mr. Hansson. These show that while Strindberg was still planning "Creditors," and before he had begun "Pariah," he had borrowed from Hansson a volume of tales by Edgar Allan Poe. It was his first acquaintance with the work of Poe, though not with American literature—for among his first printed work was a series of translations from American humourists; and not long ago a Swedish critic (Gunnar Castren in Samtiden, Christiania, June, 1912) wrote of Strindberg's literary beginnings that "he had learned much from Swedish literature, but probably more from Mark Twain and Dickens."

The impression Poe made on Strindberg was overwhelming. He returns to it in one letter after another. Everything that suits his mood of the moment is "Poesque" or "E. P.-esque." The story that seems to have made the deepest impression of all was "The Gold Bug," though his thought seems to have distilled more useful material out of certain other stories illustrating Poe's theories about mental suggestion. Under the direct influence of these theories, Strindberg, according to his own statements to Hansson, wrote the powerful one-act play "Simoom," and made Gustav in "Creditors" actually CALL FORTH the latent epileptic tendencies in Adolph. And on the same authority we must trace the method of: psychological detection practised by Mr. X. in "Pariah" directly to "The Gold Bug."

Here we have the reason why Mr. Hansson could find so little of his story in the play. And here we have the origin of a theme which, while not quite new to him, was ever afterward to remain a favourite one with Strindberg: that of a duel between intellect and cunning. It forms the basis of such novels as "Chandalah" and "At the Edge of the Sea," but it recurs in subtler form in works of much later date. To readers of the present day, Mr. X.—that striking antithesis of everything a scientist used to stand for in poetry—is much less interesting as a superman in spe than as an illustration of what a morally and mentally normal man can do with the tools furnished him by our new understanding of human ways and human motives. And in giving us a play that holds our interest as firmly as the best "love plot" ever devised, although the stage shows us only two men engaged in an intellectual wrestling match, Strindberg took another great step toward ridding the drama of its old, shackling conventions.

The name of this play has sometimes been translated as "The Outcast," whereby it becomes confused with "The Outlaw," a much earlier play on a theme from the old Sagas. I think it better, too, that the Hindu allusion in the Swedish title be not lost, for the best of men may become an outcast, but the baseness of the Pariah is not supposed to spring only from lack of social position.

PARIAH

AN ACT
1889

PERSONS
MR. X., an archaeologist, Middle-aged man.

MR. Y., an American traveller, Middle-aged man.

SCENE
(A simply furnished room in a farmhouse. The door and the windows in the background open on a landscape. In the middle of the room stands a big dining-table, covered at one end by books, writing materials, and antiquities; at the other end, by a microscope, insect cases, and specimen jars full of alchohol.)

(On the left side hangs a bookshelf. Otherwise the furniture is that of a well-to-do farmer.)

(MR. Y. enters in his shirt-sleeves, carrying a butterfly-net and a botany-can. He goes straight up to the bookshelf and takes down a book, which he begins to read on the spot.)

(The landscape outside and the room itself are steeped in sunlight. The ringing of church bells indicates that the morning services are just over. Now and then the cackling of hens is heard from the outside.)

(MR. X. enters, also in his shirt-sleeves.)

(MR. Y. starts violently, puts the book back on the shelf upside-down, and pretends to be looking for another volume.)

MR. X. This heat is horrible. I guess we are going to have a thunderstorm.

MR. Y. What makes you think so?

MR. X. The bells have a kind of dry ring to them, the flies are sticky, and the hens cackle. I meant to go fishing, but I couldn't find any worms. Don't you feel nervous?

MR. Y. [Cautiously] I?—A little.

MR. X. Well, for that matter, you always look as if you were expecting thunderstorms.

MR. Y. [With a start] Do I?

MR. X. Now, you are going away tomorrow, of course, so it is not to be wondered at that you are a little "journey-proud."— Anything new?—Oh, there's the mail! [Picks up some letters from the table] My, I have palpitation of the heart every time I open a letter! Nothing but debts, debts, debts! Have you ever had any debts?

MR. Y. [After some reflection] N-no.

MR. X. Well, then you don't know what it means to receive a lot of overdue bills. [Reads one of the letters] The rent unpaid—the landlord acting nasty—my wife in despair. And here am I sitting waist-high in gold! [He opens an iron-banded box that stands on the table; then both sit down at the table, facing each other] Just look—here I have six thousand crowns' worth of gold which I have dug up in the last fortnight. This bracelet alone would bring me the three hundred and fifty crowns I need. And with all of it I might make a fine career for myself. Then I could get the illustrations made for my treatise at once;

I could get my work printed, and—I could travel! Why don't I do it, do you suppose?

MR. Y. I suppose you are afraid to be found out.

MR. X. That, too, perhaps. But don't you think an intelligent fellow like myself might fix matters so that he was never found out? I am alone all the time—with nobody watching me—while I am digging out there in the fields. It wouldn't be strange if I put something in my own pockets now and then.

MR. Y. Yes, but the worst danger lies in disposing of the stuff.

MR. X. Pooh! I'd melt it down, of course—every bit of it—and then I'd turn it into coins—with just as much gold in them as genuine ones, of course—-

MR. Y. Of course!

MR. X. Well, you can easily see why. For if I wanted to dabble in counterfeits, then I need not go digging for gold first. [Pause] It is a strange thing anyhow, that if anybody else did what I cannot make myself do, then I'd be willing to acquit him—but I couldn't possibly acquit myself. I might even make a brilliant speech in defence of the thief, proving that this gold was res nullius, or nobody's, as it had been deposited at a time when property rights did not yet exist; that even under existing rights it could belong only to the first finder of it, as the ground-owner has never included it in the valuation of his property; and so on.

MR. Y. And probably it would be much easier for you to do this if the—hm!—the thief had not been prompted by actual need, but by a mania for collecting, for instance—or by scientific aspirations— by the ambition to keep a discovery to himself. Don't you think so?

MR. X. You mean that I could not acquit him if actual need had been the motive? Yes, for that's the only motive which the law will not accept in extenuation. That motive makes a plain theft of it.

MR. Y. And this you couldn't excuse?

MR. X. Oh, excuse—no, I guess not, as the law wouldn't. On the other hand, I must admit that it would be hard for me to charge a collector with theft merely because he had appropriated some specimen not yet represented in his own collection.

MR. Y. So that vanity or ambition might excuse what could not be excused by need?

MR. X. And yet need ought to be the more telling excuse—the only one, in fact? But I feel as I have said. And I can no more change this feeling than I can change my own determination not to steal under any circumstances whatever.

MR. Y. And I suppose you count it a great merit that you cannot— hm!—steal?

MR. X. No, my disinclination to steal is just as irresistible as the inclination to do so is irresistible with some people. So it cannot be called a merit. I cannot do it, and the other one cannot refrain!—But you understand, of course, that I am not without a desire to own this gold. Why don't I take it then? Because I cannot! It's an inability—and the lack of something cannot be called a merit. There!

[Closes the box with a slam. Stray clouds have cast their shadows on the landscape and darkened the room now and then. Now it grows quite dark as when a thunderstorm is approaching.]

MR. X. How close the air is! I guess the storm is coming all right.

[MR. Y. gets up and shuts the door and all the windows.]

MR. X. Are you afraid of thunder?

MR. Y. It's just as well to be careful.

(They resume their seats at the table.)

MR. X. You're a curious chap! Here you come dropping down like a bomb a fortnight ago, introducing yourself as a Swedish-American who is collecting flies for a small museum—-

MR. Y. Oh, never mind me now!

MR. X. That's what you always say when I grow tired of talking about myself and want to turn my attention to you. Perhaps that was the reason why I took to you as I did—because you let me talk about myself? All at once we seemed like old friends. There were no angles about you against which I could bump myself, no pins that pricked. There was something soft about your whole person, and you overflowed with that tact which only well-educated people know how to show. You never made a noise when you came home late at night or got up early in the morning. You were patient in small things, and you gave in whenever a conflict seemed threatening. In a word, you proved yourself the perfect companion! But you were entirely too compliant not to set me wondering about you in the long run—and you are too timid, too easily frightened. It seems almost as if you were made up of two different personalities. Why, as I sit here looking at your back in the mirror over there—it is as if I were looking at somebody else.

(MR. Y. turns around and stares at the mirror.)

MR. X. No, you cannot get a glimpse of your own back, man!—In front you appear like a fearless sort of fellow, one meeting his fate with bared breast, but from behind—really, I don't want to be impolite, but—you look as if you were carrying a burden, or as if you were crouching to escape a raised stick. And when I look at that red cross your suspenders make on your white shirt—well, it looks to me like some kind of emblem, like a trade-mark on a packing-box—

MR. Y. I feel as if I'd choke— if the storm doesn't break soon—

MR. X. It's coming—don't you worry!—And your neck! It looks as if there ought to be another kind of face on top of it, a face quite different in type from yours. And your ears come so close together behind that sometimes I wonder what race you belong to. [A flash of lightning lights up the room] Why, it looked as if that might have struck the sheriff's house!

MR. Y. [Alarmed] The sheriff's

MR. X. Oh, it just looked that way. But I don't think we'll get much of this storm. Sit down now and let us have a talk, as you are going away to-morrow. One thing I find strange is that you, with whom I have become so intimate in this short time—that you are one of those whose image I cannot call up when I am away from them. When you are not here, and I happen to think of you, I always get the vision of another acquaintance—one who does not resemble you, but with whom you have certain traits in common.

MR. Y. Who is he?

MR. X. I don't want to name him, but—I used for several years to take my meals at a certain place, and there, at the side-table where they kept the whiskey and the otter preliminaries, I met a little blond man, with blond, faded eyes. He had a wonderful faculty for making his way through a crowd, without jostling anybody or being jostled himself. And from his customary place down by the door he seemed perfectly able to reach whatever he wanted on a table that stood some six feet away from him. He seemed always happy just to be in company. But when he met anybody he knew, then the joy of it made him roar with laughter, and he would hug and pat the other fellow as if he hadn't seen a human face for years. When anybody stepped on his foot, he smiled as if eager to apologise for being in the way. For two years I watched him and amused myself by guessing at his occupation and character. But I never asked who he was; I didn't want to know, you see, for then all the fun would have been spoiled at once. That man had just your quality of being indefinite. At different times I made him out to be a teacher who had never got his licence, a non- commissioned officer, a druggist, a government clerk, a detective- -and like you, he looked as if made out of two pieces, for the front of him never quite fitted the back. One day I happened to read in a newspaper about a big forgery committed by a well-known government official. Then I learned that my indefinite gentleman had been a partner of the forger's brother, and that his name was Strawman. Later on I learned that the aforesaid Strawman used to run a circulating library, but that he was now the police reporter of a big daily. How in the world could I hope to establish a connection between the forgery, the police, and my little man's peculiar manners? It was beyond me; and when I asked a friend whether Strawman had ever been punished for something, my friend couldn't answer either yes or no—he just didn't know! [Pause.]

MR. Y. Well, had he ever been—punished?

MR. X. No, he had not. [Pause.]

MR. Y. And that was the reason, you think, why the police had such an attraction for him, and why he was so afraid of offending people?

MR. X. Exactly!

MR. Y. And did you become acquainted with him afterward?

MR. X. No, I didn't want to. [Pause.]

MR. Y. Would you have been willing to make his acquaintance if he had been—punished?

MR. X. Perfectly!

(MR. Y. rises and walks back and forth several times.)

MR. X. Sit still! Why can't you sit still?

MR. Y. How did you get your liberal view of human conditions? Are you a Christian?

MR. X. Oh, can't you see that I am not?

(MR. Y. makes a face.)

MR. X. The Christians require forgiveness. But I require punishment in order that the balance, or whatever you may call it, be restored. And you, who have served a term, ought to know the difference.

MR. Y. [Stands motionless and stares at MR. X., first with wild, hateful eyes, then with surprise and admiration] How—could—you- -know—that?

MR. X. Why, I could see it.

MR. Y. How? How could you see it?

MR. X, Oh, with a little practice. It is an art, like many others. But don't let us talk of it any more. [He looks at his watch, arranges a document on the table, dips a pen in the ink-well, and hands it to MR. Y.] I must be thinking of my tangled affairs. Won't you please witness my signature on this note here? I am going to turn it in to the bank at Malmo tomorrow, when I go to the city with you.

MR. Y. I am not going by way of Malmo.

MR. X. Oh, you are not?

MR. Y. No.

MR. X. But that need not prevent you from witnessing my signature.

MR. Y. N-no!—I never write my name on papers of that kind—

MR. X.—any longer! This is the fifth time you have refused to write your own name. The first time nothing more serious was involved than the receipt for a registered letter. Then I began to watch you. And since then I have noticed that you have a morbid fear of a pen filled with ink. You have not written a single letter since you came here—only a postcard, and that you wrote with a blue pencil. You understand now that I have figured out the exact nature of your slip? Furthermore! This is something like the seventh time you have refused to come with me to Malmo, which place you have not visited at all during all this time. And yet you came the whole way from America merely to have a look at Malmo! And every morning you walk a couple of miles, up to the old mill, just to get a glimpse of the roofs of Malmo in the distance. And when you stand over there at the right-hand window and look out through the third pane from the bottom on the left side, you can see the spired turrets of the castle and the tall chimney of the county jail.—And now I hope you see that it's your own stupidity rather than my cleverness which has made everything clear to me.

MR. Y. This means that you despise me?

MR. X. Oh, no!

MR. Y. Yes, you do—you cannot but do it!

MR. X. No—here's my hand.

(MR. Y. takes hold of the outstretched hand and kisses it.)

MR. X. [Drawing back his hand] Don't lick hands like a dog!

MR. Y. Pardon me, sir, but you are the first one who has let me touch his hand after learning—

MR. X. And now you call me "sir!"—What scares me about you is that you don't feel exonerated, washed clean, raised to the old level, as good as anybody else, when you have suffered your punishment. Do you care to tell me how it happened? Would you?

MR. Y. [Twisting uneasily] Yes, but you won't believe what I say. But I'll tell you. Then you can see for yourself that I am no ORDINARY criminal. You'll become convinced, I think, that there are errors which, so to speak, are involuntary—[twisting again] which seem to commit themselves—spontaneously—without being willed by oneself, and for which one cannot be held responsible— May I open the door a little now, since the storm seems to have passed over?

MR. X. Suit yourself.

MR. Y. [Opens the door; then he sits down at the table and begins to speak with exaggerated display of feeling, theatrical gestures, and a good deal of false emphasis] Yes, I'll tell you! I was a student in the university at Lund, and I needed to get a loan from a bank. I had no pressing debts, and my father owned some property—not a great deal, of course. However, I had sent the note to the second man of the two who were to act as security, and, contrary to expectations, it came back with a refusal. For a while I was completely stunned by the blow, for it was a very unpleasant surprise—most unpleasant! The note was lying in front of me on the table, and the letter lay beside it. At first my eyes stared hopelessly at those lines that pronounced my doom—that is, not a death-doom, of course, for I could easily find other securities, as many as I wanted—but as I have already said, it was very annoying just the same. And as I was sitting there quite unconscious of any evil intention, my eyes fastened upon the signature of the letter, which would have made my future secure if it had only appeared in the right place. It was an unusually well-written signature—and you know how sometimes one may absent-mindedly scribble a sheet of paper full of meaningless words. I had a pen in my hand—[picks up a penholder from the table] like this. And somehow it just began to run—I don't want to claim that there was anything mystical—anything of a spiritualistic nature back of it—for that kind of thing I don't believe in! It was a wholly unreasoned, mechanical process—my copying of that beautiful autograph over and over again. When all the clean space on the letter was used up, I had learned to reproduce the signature automatically—and then—[throwing away the penholder with a violent gesture] then I forgot all about it. That night I slept long and heavily. And when I woke up, I could feel that I had been dreaming, but I couldn't recall the dream itself. At times it was as if a door had been thrown ajar, and then I seemed to see the writing-table with the note on it as in a distant memory—and when I got out of bed, I was forced up to the table, just as if, after careful deliberation, I had formed an irrevocable decision to sign the name to that fateful paper. All thought of the consequences, of the risk involved, had disappeared—no hesitation remained—it was almost as if I was fulfilling some sacred duty—and so I wrote! [Leaps to his feet] What could it be? Was it some kind of outside influence, a case of mental suggestion, as they call it? But from whom could it come? I was sleeping alone in that room. Could it possibly be my primitive self—the savage to whom the keeping of faith is an unknown thing--which pushed to the front while my consciousness was asleep— together with the criminal will of that self, and its inability to calculate the results of an action? Tell me, what do you think of it?

MR. X. [As if he had to force the words out of himself] Frankly speaking, your story does not convince me—there are gaps in it, but these may depend on your failure to recall all the details—and I have read something about criminal suggestion—or I think I have, at least—hm! But all that is neither here nor there! You have taken your medicine—and you have had the courage to acknowledge your fault. Now we won't talk of it any more.

MR. Y. Yes, yes, yes, we must talk of it—till I become sure of my innocence.

MR. X. Well, are you not?

MR. Y. No, I am not!

MR. X. That's just what bothers me, I tell you It's exactly what is bothering me!—Don't you feel fairly sure that every human being hides a skeleton in his closet? Have we not, all of us, stolen and lied as children? Undoubtedly! Well, now there are persons who remain children all their lives, so that they cannot control their unlawful desires. Then comes the opportunity, and there you have your criminal.—But I cannot understand why you don't feel innocent. If the child is not held responsible why should the criminal be regarded differently? It is the more strange because—well, perhaps I may come to repent it later. [Pause] I, for my part, have killed a man, and I have never suffered any qualms on account of it.

MR. Y. [Very much interested] Have—you?

MR. X. Yes, I, and none else! Perhaps you don't care to shake hands with a murderer?

MR. Y. [Pleasantly] Oh, what nonsense

MR. X. Yes, but I have not been punished.

MR. Y. [Growing more familiar and taking on a superior tone] So much the better for you!—How did you get out of it?

MR. X. There was nobody to accuse me, no suspicions, no witnesses. This is the way it happened. One Christmas I was invited to hunt with a fellow-student a little way out of Upsala. He sent a besotted old coachman to meet me at the station, and this fellow went to sleep on the box, drove the horses into a fence, and upset the whole equipage in a ditch. I am not going to pretend that my life was in danger. It was sheer impatience which made me hit him across the neck with the edge of my hand—you know the way—just to wake him up—and the result was that he never woke up at all, but collapsed there and there.

MR. Y. [Craftily] And did you report it?

MR. X. No, and these were my reasons for not doing so. The man left no family behind him, or anybody else to whom his life could be of the slightest use. He had already outlived his allotted period of vegetation, and his place might just as well be filled by somebody more in need of it. On the other hand, my life was necessary to the happiness of my parents and myself, and perhaps also to the progress of my science. The outcome had once for all cured me of any desire to wake up people in that manner, and I didn't care to spoil both my own life and that of my parents for the sake of an abstract principle of justice.

MR. Y. Oh, that's the way you measure the value of a human life?

MR. X. In the present case, yes.

MR. Y. But the sense of guilt—that balance you were speaking of?

MR. X. I had no sense of guilt, as I had committed no crime. As a boy I had given and taken more than one blow of the same kind, and the fatal outcome in this particular case was simply caused by my ignorance of the effect such a blow might have on an elderly person.

MR. Y. Yes, but even the unintentional killing of a man is punished with a two-year term at hard labour—which is exactly what one gets for—writing names.

MR. X. Oh, you may be sure I have thought of it. And more than one night I have dreamt myself in prison. Tell me now—is it really as bad as they say to find oneself behind bolt and bar?

MR. Y. You bet it is!—First of all they disfigure you by cutting off your hair, and if you don't look like a criminal before, you are sure to do so afterward. And when you catch sight of yourself in a mirror you feel quite sure that you are a regular bandit.

MR. X. Isn't it a mask that is being torn off, perhaps? Which wouldn't be a bad idea, I should say.

MR. Y. Yes, you can have your little jest about it!—And then they cut down your food, so that every day and every hour you become conscious of the border line between life and death. Every vital function is more or less checked. You can feel yourself shrinking. And your soul, which was to be cured and improved, is instead put on a starvation diet—pushed back a thousand years into outlived ages. You are not permitted to read anything but what was written for the savages who took part in the migration of the peoples. You hear of nothing but what will never happen in heaven; and what actually does happen on the earth is kept hidden from you. You are torn out of your surroundings, reduced from your own class, put beneath those who are really beneath yourself. Then you get a sense of living in the bronze age. You come to feel as if you were dressed in skins, as if you were living in a cave and eating out of a trough—ugh!

MR. X. But there is reason back of all that. One who acts as if he belonged to the bronze age might surely be expected to don the proper costume.

MR. Y. [Irately] Yes, you sneer! You who have behaved like a man from the stone age—and who are permitted to live in the golden age.

MR. X. [Sharply, watching him closely] What do you mean with that last expression—the golden age?

MR. Y. [With a poorly suppressed snarl] Nothing at all.

MR. X. Now you lie—because you are too much of a coward to say all you think.

MR. Y. Am I a coward? You think so? But I was no coward when I dared to show myself around here, where I had had to suffer as I did.—But can you tell what makes one suffer most while in there?- -It is that the others are not in there too!

MR. X. What others?

MR. Y. Those that go unpunished.

MR. X. Are you thinking of me?

MR. Y. I am.

MR. X. But I have committed no crime.

MR. Y. Oh, haven't you?

MR. X. No, a misfortune is no crime.

MR. Y. So, it's a misfortune to commit murder?

MR. X. I have not committed murder.

MR. Y. Is it not murder to kill a person?

MR. X. Not always. The law speaks of murder, manslaughter, killing in self-defence—and it makes a distinction between intentional and unintentional killing. However—now you really frighten me, for it's becoming plain to me that you belong to the most dangerous of all human groups—that of the stupid.

MR. Y. So you imagine that I am stupid? Well, listen—would you like me to show you how clever I am?

MR. X. Come on!

MR. Y. I think you'll have to admit that there is both logic and wisdom in the argument I'm now going to give you. You have suffered a misfortune which might have brought you two years at hard labor. You have completely escaped the disgrace of being punished. And here you see before you a man—who has also suffered a misfortune—the victim of an unconscious impulse—and who has had to stand two years of hard labor for it. Only by some great scientific achievement can this man wipe off the taint that has become attached to him without any fault of his own—but in order to arrive at some such achievement, he must have money—a lot of money—and money this minute! Don't you think that the other one, the unpunished one, would bring a little better balance into these unequal human conditions if he paid a penalty in the form of a fine? Don't you think so?

MR. X. [Calmly] Yes.

MR. Y. Then we understand each other.—Hm! [Pause] What do you think would be reasonable?

MR. X. Reasonable? The minimum fine in such a case is fixed by the law at fifty crowns. But this whole question is settled by the fact that the dead man left no relatives.

MR. Y. Apparently you don't want to understand. Then I'll have to speak plainly: it is to me you must pay that fine.

MR. X. I have never heard that forgers have the right to collect fines imposed for manslaughter. And, besides, there is no prosecutor.

MR. Y. There isn't? Well—how would I do?

MR. X. Oh, NOW we are getting the matter cleared up! How much do you want for becoming my accomplice?

MR. Y. Six thousand crowns.

MR. X. That's too much. And where am I to get them?

(MR. Y. points to the box.)

MR. X. No, I don't want to do that. I don't want to become a thief.

MR. Y. Oh, don't put on any airs now! Do you think I'll believe that you haven't helped yourself out of that box before?

MR. X. [As if speaking to himself] Think only, that I could let myself be fooled so completely. But that's the way with these soft natures. You like them, and then it's so easy to believe that they like you. And that's the reason why I have always been on my guard against people I take a liking to!—So you are firmly convinced that I have helped myself out of the box before?

MR. Y. Certainly! MR. X. And you are going to report me if you don't get six thousand crowns?

MR. Y. Most decidedly! You can't get out of it, so there's no use trying.

MR. X. You think I am going to give my father a thief for son, my wife a thief for husband, my children a thief for father, my fellow-workers a thief for colleague? No, that will never happen!- - Now I am going over to the sheriff to report the killing myself.

MR. Y. [Jumps up and begins to pick up his things] Wait a moment!

MR. X. For what?

MR. Y. [Stammering] Oh, I thought—as I am no longer needed—it wouldn't be necessary for me to stay—and I might just as well leave.

MR. X. No, you may not!—Sit down there at the table, where you sat before, and we'll have another talk before you go.

MR. Y. [Sits down after having put on a dark coat] What are you up to now?

MR. X. [Looking into the mirror back of MR. Y.] Oh, now I have it! Oh-h-h!

MR. Y. [Alarmed] What kind of wonderful things are you discovering now?

MR. X. I see in the mirror that you are a thief—a plain, ordinary thief! A moment ago, while you had only the white shirt on, I could notice that there was something wrong about my bookshelf. I couldn't make out just what it was, for I had to listen to you and watch you. But as my antipathy increased, my vision became more acute. And now, with your black coat to furnish the needed color contrast For the red back of the book, which before couldn't be seen against the red of your suspenders—now I see that you have been reading about forgeries in Bernheim's work on mental suggestion—for you turned the book upsidedown in putting it back. So even that story of yours was stolen! For tins reason I think myself entitled to conclude that your crime must have been prompted by need, or by mere love of pleasure.

MR. Y. By need! If you only knew—

MR. X. If YOU only knew the extent of the need I have had to face and live through! But that's another story! Let's proceed with your case. That you have been in prison—I take that for granted. But it happened in America, for it was American prison life you described. Another thing may also be taken for granted, namely, that you have not borne your punishment on this side.

MR. Y. How can you imagine anything of the kind?

MR. X. Wait until the sheriff gets here, and you'll learn all about it.

(MR. Y. gets up.)

MR. X. There you see! The first time I mentioned the sheriff, in connection with the storm, you wanted also to run away. And when a person has served out his time he doesn't care to visit an old mill every day just to look at a prison, or to stand by the window—in a word, you are at once punished and unpunished. And that's why it was so hard to make you out. [Pause.]

MR. Y. [Completely beaten] May I go now?

MR. X. Now you can go.

MR. Y. [Putting his things together] Are you angry at me?

MR. X. Yes—would you prefer me to pity you?

MR. Y. [Sulkily] Pity? Do you think you're any better than I?

MR. X. Of course I do, as I AM better than you. I am wiser, and I am less of a menace to prevailing property rights.

MR. Y. You think you are clever, but perhaps I am as clever as you. For the moment you have me checked, but in the next move I can mate you—all the same!

MR. X. [Looking hard at MR. Y.] So we have to have another bout! What kind of mischief are you up to now?

MR. Y. That's my secret.

MR. X. Just look at me—oh, you mean to write my wife an anonymous letter giving away MY secret!

MR. Y. Well, how are you going to prevent it? You don't care to have me arrested. So you'll have to let me go. And when I am gone, I can do what I please.

MR. X. You devil! So you have found my vulnerable spot! Do you want to make a real murderer out of me?

MR. Y. That's more than you'll ever become—coward!

MR. X. There you see how different people are. You have a feeling that I cannot become guilty of the same kind of acts as you. And that gives you the upper hand. But suppose you forced me to treat you as I treated that coachman?

[He lifts his hand as if ready to hit MR. Y.]

MR. Y. [Staring MR. X. straight in the face] You can't! It's too much for one who couldn't save himself by means of the box over there.

MR. X. So you don't think I have taken anything out of the box?

MR. Y. You were too cowardly—just as you were too cowardly to tell your wife that she had married a murderer.

MR. X. You are a different man from what I took you to be—if stronger or weaker, I cannot tell—if more criminal or less, that's none of my concern—but decidedly more stupid; that much is quite plain. For stupid you were when you wrote another person's name instead of begging—as I have had to do. Stupid you were when you stole things out of my book—could you not guess that I might have read my own books? Stupid you were when you thought yourself cleverer than me, and when you thought that I could be lured into becoming a thief. Stupid you were when you thought balance could be restored by giving the world two thieves instead of one. But most stupid of all you were when you thought I had failed to provide a safe corner-stone for my happiness. Go ahead and write my wife as many anonymous letters as you please about her husband having killed a man—she knew that long before we were married!— Have you had enough now?

MR. Y. May I go?

MR. X. Now you HAVE to go! And at once! I'll send your things after you!—Get out of here!

(Curtain.)

***